—An International Survey of—

ROCKING HORSE MANUFACTURE

Marguerite Fawdry

CONTENTS

NEW CAVENDISH BOOKS

ACKNOWLEDGEMENTS

My thanks to all the museums and their staff, manufacturers, collectors and friends who have helped towards the realization of this survey.

FRONT COVER

ABOVE LEFT Carousel horse on rockers from Halifax, Nova Scotia. (National Museum of Canada) Canada)

ABOVE RIGHT Painted wooden horse from Gorodets.

BELOW LEFT Horse on cradle rockers, 1930. (Baden Kinder Museum)

BELOW RIGHT Horse made in northern Thailand for export, 1990. Length: 39in. (99cm). Height: 23in. (58.5cm).

BACK COVER Mameluke, General and officer. Watercolour of wheeled wooden toy horses from Histoire des Jouets by H R d'Allemagne, 1903. (British Library)

This book is only available in conjunction with The Rocking Horse – A History of Moving Toy Horses by Patricia Mullins.

First edition published in Great Britain by New Cavendish Books – 1992

Designed by Jacky Wedgwood

Edited by Narisa Chakra

Typeset by Wyvern Typesetting Limited, Bristol

Printed and bound in China under the supervision of Mandarin Offset, London

New Cavendish Books 3 Denbigh Road, London W11 2SJ

ISBN 1 872727 06 9

Introduction

This survey grew out of notes originally compiled for a projected third edition of *A History of Rocking Horses* to be published by Pollock's. In the meantime, New Cavendish Books suggested they would make an interesting supplement to Patricia Mullins' book.

The reference files on rocking horses at Pollock's Toy Museum from which much of this material is drawn have grown over the years. Yet even though they take up more and more shelf space there are still gaps to be filled and questions to be answered. Were the basket weave peasant rocking horses, for example, which I saw in a Balkan market long ago, from Rumania or nearby Yugoslavia? In which Bavarian town did I see a young man sitting on the pavement next to some beautiful horses he had made? Why on that quiet summer evening in the fields by the ruins of Troy did I not pay more attention to the crude little horses on sale there while my mind turned instead to the magnificent steed depicted in Orlando Hodgson's toy theatre play 'The Giant Horse'? Did the 'Pasha' horse, now in the Carolina Augusteum Museum in Vienna, come perhaps from the same stable as those 'trojan' ones?

And there are geographical problems as well. With all the changes in the map of Europe since the First World War how does one classify the origins of certain rocking horse makes and manufacturers? At the time when many of the horses were made many of the present-day states did not exist. Furthermore in the current climate of political upheaval does Europe still end at the Bosphorus? At the end of this supplement under the heading 'Old Horses at Rest' are the names of museums in Britain, Europe and North America which have rocking horses in their collections. The list has been subdivided into present day national states though the horses do not fit conveniently into those national boundaries. Rocking horses have always been widely exported and are well-travelled beasts. Thus there are German horses which have strayed far from the Thuringian forests where they were conceived, an English 'Nobs' metal horse resides in Switzerland, a Canadian one in Germany, and French tricycle horses travel to Bavaria and the Netherlands. To avoid too many historical complications all the European horses have been grouped within their twentieth century national frontiers.

'Pasha' horse from Anatolia Turkey, twentieth century. (Salzburg Carolina Augusteum Museum)

Siege of Troy. Orlando Hodgson, 1833. (Reprint Pollock's Toy Theatres, 1985)

Wooden horse in the Royal Palace, Aranjuez. (El Juquete en España)

ABOVE RIGHT *A beechwood horse with wooden eyes made on the outskirts of Strasbourg, early nineteenth century. (Musée Alsacien)*

Horse with carved wood tail, made by Andreas Bienz, Basel. 1826. (Basel Historisches Museum, Switzerland)

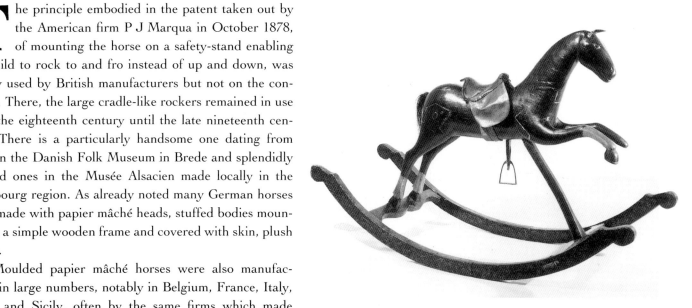

he principle embodied in the patent taken out by the American firm P J Marqua in October 1878, of mounting the horse on a safety-stand enabling the child to rock to and fro instead of up and down, was widely used by British manufacturers but not on the continent. There, the large cradle-like rockers remained in use from the eighteenth century until the late nineteenth century. There is a particularly handsome one dating from 1778 in the Danish Folk Museum in Brede and splendidly painted ones in the Musée Alsacien made locally in the Strasbourg region. As already noted many German horses were made with papier mâché heads, stuffed bodies mounted on a simple wooden frame and covered with skin, plush or felt.

Moulded papier mâché horses were also manufactured in large numbers, notably in Belgium, France, Italy, Spain and Sicily, often by the same firms which made carnival masks and large figures for religious processions.

These papier mâché horses were usually painted white with very large stylised spots. Wooden horses produced in peasant kitchens during the long snow bound winter days in high Alpine villages, appeared in the spring covered with a riot of bright mountain flowers.

British and North American horses stand squarely on their rockers either in a standing position or with limbs outstretched in a gallop. In contrast, many German and Scandinavian horses high step more elegantly one foreleg off the ground in the manner of antique equestrian statues. Other horses are carved rearing up on their back legs with only a central metal or wood pivot on which they balance. In Kavlas castle, Sweden, there is still a magnificent beast made for King Charles XII, and another in Palacio Real de Aranjuez Spain. From their appearance these huge cavalry horses would seem to be more at home in a noble armoury than in a prince's nursery.

Another military echo is found in the carved wooden docked bobtails of horses found in German, Swiss and Austrian museums.

In March 1990 an envelope from Vienna arrived at Pollock's Toy Museum. It contained photographs, newspaper cuttings and a letter from Ferdinand Bauer:

"Following in the footsteps of my grandfather and father, I have made rocking horses for the past 56 years. Only in a small way nowadays as I am actively involved with the Museum of Art History in Vienna. I am retired but still look after my horses in the workshop. I also do repairs. . . ."

"At the beginning of the year the wood arrives. It is cut, glued and rounded up. In the summer the torsos are hung from the ceiling. In the autumn they are sand-papered, painted and harnessed."

Ferdinand Bauer was 14 years old when he began working with his father. His grandfather began making horses in 1906. At that time his grandfather was working at a nearby arms factory. The workers were allowed to take home the wooden crates. Instead of using this timber, like his workmates to heat the kitchen stove, the whole family used it to make horses in a small workshop which they rented. Eventually Ferdinand's father took over the business, employing 10 workers in 1928 and trying to modernise the classic models by using new materials and simplifying the production. In 1948 Ferdinand returned from a prisoner-of-war camp in Russia. Vienna was in chaos. Gradually the workshop was set to rights and a

decision was taken to buy a ten-ton press and steam-mould the horses out of sheets of hardwood. Soon he was employing three other workers and turning out 1500 horses a year.

Hard times returned however as plastics took over the toy market and Ferdinand Bauer had to take a job with the Museum of Art History in Vienna. When he retired, he still had his workshop and started to make a few wooden horses as he had done in his youth. Today he enjoys a modest success, as his hand-carved horses are once more in demand. In addition to the Ferdinand Bauer workshop, two other Austrian firms are currently making horses.

The low vaulted rooms of the old Carolina Augusteum Palace in central Vienna now house the collection of Austrian and other folk toys which Hugo and Gabriele Folk-Stoi built up twenty years ago. Among them is a charming donkey carved in the eighteenth century for a church tableau – the humble ass, which, on Palm Sunday carried Jesus on his back. From this exalted role, the patient animal became a nursery toy or was used for punishing dunces in nursery schools.

Ferdinand Bauer in his workshop. (Photo: Ernst Hausner)

ABOVE *Carved wooden donkey, made for Palm Sunday processions and later adapted for use as a toy. Austrian, eighteenth century. (Salzburg Carolina Augusteum Museum)*

LEFT *Rocking horse by Ferdinand Bauer. Vienna, twentieth century.*

Larger skin-covered horse on wheeled platform, early nineteenth century. Smaller horse on bow rockers, stuffed body, covered with jute, carved head with glass eyes (head detail below). Vienna, c. 1860. (Salzburg Carolina Augusteum Museum)

It is often difficult to determine whether the rocking horses were made in Austria or imported from Germany, which was the largest manufacturer of wooden toys in the nineteenth century. The examples illustrated have been sent in to Pollocks from the Salzburg Carolina Augusteum Museum and the Tiroler Volkskunst Museum.

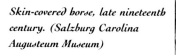

Rocking chair, nineteenth century. (Salzburg Carolina Augusteum Museum). Head detail right

Skin-covered horse, late nineteenth century. (Salzburg Carolina Augusteum Museum)

Wooden horse with carved bobtail. Carved in Ausserfern first half of the nineteenth century. Length: 50in. (125cm). Height: 39in. (87cm). (Tiroler Volkskunst Museum)

From the end of the last century to the beginning of the Second World War the town of Deinze was the centre of large-scale toy making in Belgium. One of the biggest firms was that of Nazaire Beeusaert who made wheeled papier mâché horses in a large range of models and sizes from 15cm to 1 metre high. The horses were moulded in two halves, dried, stuck together and either painted or covered with felt. Large numbers were exported and in co-operation with another local firm, Desiré Dierick, horse heads were fixed to rocking chairs and tricycles.

The firm of Nazaire Beeusaert made forts, farmyards, dolls cradles and, under the trade mark 'N B', trenches and toy soldiers moulded out of paper, chalk and glue. They also distributed the 'Batima' construction sets from 1930 until overtaken by the success of 'Lego' plastic building bricks. The firm still exists but they no longer make toys.

Several Dutch museums have toys in their collections. In the opinion of their curators it would seem that rocking horses were not popular in Holland and were never made there. The few which do exist were all imported. This would in all probability also apply to the two-legged hobby horses shown in an engraving of a market stall, dated 1616, and of another depicting a fairground tent with a large vaulting horse on which acrobatic feats are being performed.

Papier mâché pull-along horse by Nazaire Beeusaert, c. 1910.
(Les Jouets en Belgique)

The range of papier mâché wheeled horses by Nazaire Beeusaert.
(Les Jouets en Belgique)

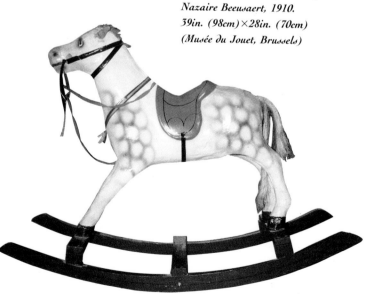

Papier mâché rocking horse by Nazaire Beeusaert, 1910.
39in. (98cm)×28in. (70cm)
(Musée du Jouet, Brussels)

French Book of Hours, early sixteenth century. (Bodleian Library)

ABOVE RIGHT *Lithograph from a drawing by J Condé (1813) of Napoleon I's son, the Duc de Reichstadt, from* Histoire des Jouets *by H R d'Allemagne, 1903. (British Library)*

To relieve the boredom of endlessly copying the Holy Scriptures by hand, medieval monks would enliven the manuscript's margins with borders of flowers, birds and beasts, golden flourishes and scenes from daily life. An early sixteenth century French Book of Hours, now in the Bodleian Library, Oxford, recounts the story of St Martin who gave up his life as a soldier to become Bishop of Tours in the year 400 and ultimately a saint for having one day shared his cloak with a beggar. At the bottom of the page three small boys are dashing around the garden, riding their hobby-horses under the watchful eye of their nurse or mother. The horses are beautifully made, even though all that is needed to play at horses is a stick and a little imagination and as children have been doing since ancient times.

In his satirical masterpiece *Gargantua and Pontaguel*, published in 1534, Rabelais describes the upbringing of the giant King and describes the horses he made from a large oak beam. Gargantua made a horse for hunting from a wine press and a hack for use every day from a large block of oak; also a horse which could rear and jump as well as a mule and its harness plus a stable of smaller horses.

Early nineteenth century French engravings show boys riding rocking horses and hobby-horses. The earliest pictures of a horse on bow rockers is a drawing by

J Condé, dated 1813. The horse is being ridden by the two year old son of Napoleon I. Was this horse made in France, or in Austria or in Germany? We do not know. The boy's mother was an Austrian princess and after the battle of Waterloo, the little prince was hustled off to his grandfather's palace in Shoenbraun, where he spent the rest of his short life.

The epitome of French elegance is perhaps a beautiful silk scarf and a discreet leather hand bag from Hermès in the Faubourg St Honoré. This firm has been renowned since 1837, for its hand-made saddles and leather goods and more recently for luxury silks, scent and porcelain. Two toy horses reside in the headquarters of this world-wide empire of two thousand shops. One is a family heirloom; an English-made horse, which has been in the showroom since 1880. The other, perhaps the most romantic toy in France, is a tricycle horse which belonged to Eugène, Louis Jean Joseph Napoleon, Prince Imperial (1856–1879), Napoleon III's only son. The horse is beautifully carved, covered in skin, the leather harness and handle bars are stamped with the letter N surmounted by a crown, the velvet saddle cloth is fringed with gold. The wheels are well-made with iron rims. The prince played with it for a year or two, then gave it to a member of his palace staff. After the defeat of 1870 came the years of exile in England, the military Academy of Sandhurst and death at the age of 23 in South Africa, when he was killed in battle fighting the Zulus.

A neglected monument in the woods of Chislehurst Common not far from the house where his mother the Empress Eugénie lived out the long years of her widowhood and the pretty horse in the Paris show-room are all that remains to remind us of this brave young prince.

In the Nathan Cummings Collection in Chicago is a light-hearted painting by Claude Monet of his son Jean riding a tricycle horse. In 1872, the year in which the picture was painted, tricycle horses were one of the most popular toys in France. Uncertain weather perhaps played its part in restricting the rocking horse in England to the nursery, whilst French children had more opportunities for playing outside in the garden and dashing around on velocipedes and tricycles. Interest in the development of the bicycle has always been of importance in France. As early as 1791 Count Sivrac was scooting round the gardens of the Palais Royal on a two-wheeled contraption. In 1820, Nicephore Niepce, the world's first photographer was demonstrating his improved version in the Luxembourg Gardens. In 1822 Messiers Courbé and Gourdoux were respectively taking out patents for tricycle horses whose back wheels turned by chain wheel drive worked by handles each side of the horse's head. In 1852 came velocipedes worked by pedals. The Michaux Brothers opened their factory in 1861 for the manufacture of perambulators, tricycles, and pedal bicycles. 1869 saw the first safety bicycle with wire spoked wheels, rubber tyres and chain driven back wheels, exhibited at the first Paris Bicycle Show.

Tricycle horse given to Napoleon III's son, Eugène (1856–79). (Collection Hermès)

A Garnier tricycle horse, second half of the nineteenth century. (Simon van Gign Museum, Dordrecht)

OPPOSITE PAGE

LEFT *The Hunt – a game with carved wooden figures from* Recreations et Passetemps *by H R d'Allemagne, 1906. (British Library)*

RIGHT *Rocking horse with wheels, c. 1900. (Musée du Jouet, Poissy)*

RIGHT *Wheeled horse made by Gustave Bayol for his daughter, Mireille, 1904–05. Height to saddle: approx 10in. (25cm). (Monsieur Charles Gilbert)*

Wooden fretwork stable by G Lenoble, sold at Christie's, 1990.

BELOW RIGHT *Lenoble catalogue, c. 1910. (Wicki Schweizer)*

Wooden horse made in Strasbourg for the Bergmann family in 1860, pinewood rockers, hard wood head. Length: 50in. (125cm). Height: 28½in. (71cm). (Musée Alsacien)

Charles Gilbert, the editor of *L'Anjou*, the Angers local daily newspaper, has spent many years researching the history of Gustave Bayol, the famous carver of horses and other animals for merry-go-rounds who worked in Angers. He has interviewed all the surviving members of the Bayol family. When asked if he thought Gustave Bayol had also made rocking horses for the toyshop he opened after the First World War, he replied: "Although a rocking horse is illustrated on a publicity postcard printed between 1906–1910, it would seem that Bayol did not produce any rocking horses. This type of horse was not very popular at that time – pull- and push-along horses were more in demand. Bayol made three sizes in his workshops. The most beautiful one was made in 1905 for his daughter Mireille and is still owned by the Bayol family."

Charles Gilbert's assertion that rocking horses were not in great demand in France is probably true. Rocking horses, however, were made and bought by some rich families during the nineteenth and earth twentieth centuries. The two principal centres for their manufacture were Alsace and the Jura mountains where timber was plentiful and the inhabitants were skilled in the manufacture of turned wooden wares.

The horses in the Musée Alsacien in Strasbourg were all made locally and date from the end of the eighteenth century to late nineteeth century. Like the horses in

neighbouring Germany, they are mounted on large cradle rockers, or like fairground horses they prance up on their hind legs, supported by a central post (see p. 4).

Further south in the Jura mountains, local craftsmen and small workshops produced a wide range of household goods, farm implements, toys, dominoes, chess sets and counters for board games.

Two firms near Moirans-en-Montagne made and still make rocking horses. The first is L'Arbre à Jouer, founded in 1870 and still producing two styles of very simplified beechwood rocking horses. Clairbois, formerly Clerc-Clairbois and now part of the Superjouet group, produces plush-covered horses on metal or wooden rockers, mostly convertible to wheeled toys. Other firms in the region such as Giraud-Sauveur founded in 1910 also made traditional

wooden horses, until the 1950s when moulded plastic took over.

Lenoble, at Senlis near Paris, made wooden rocking horses and stables for smaller horses in the 1920s. Between 1900 and the 1930s, at Crevecoeur-le-Grand, the firm of Clerc and Sons produced wooden horses as well as moulded papier mâché horses, patterned all over by large distinctive brown spots. The local mayor, Pierre Varlet, explained how the horses were made, mostly by young women workers: "Sheets of cardboard were cut to fit the two sides of the mould. When they were shaped, they were taken out, stapled together and coated. The legs were made in the factory from a mixture of glues and powder built up around metal supports. There was a wide range of models. Some were varnished others painted in different colours or covered with calf-skin." A horse from the Clerc factory can be seen in the toy museum at Poissy.

Between 1980 and 1987, the English director of Les Jouets Taiga, marketed some large horses carved from lime wood with real horsehair manes, mounted on safety rockers. The demand for these expensive English-type horses was limited and production stopped.

Today the amusing rocking grasshoppers, insects, animals and horses made by the firm 'La Sauterelle' from different coloured woods are more to the taste of French buyers. The most beautiful are perhaps the horses, made to order by the sculptor Remy Serret who carves them from local walnut, lime, or cypress woods.

Limewood horse by Remy Serret, 1990. Length: rockers 44in. (110cm), body 26in. (65cm).

Wooden horse by Sauterelle, 1990. Height to saddle: 25in. (63cm). Length: 64in. (160cm).

Christmas card, c. 1900. (Spielzeug und Kinderwelt Museum, Steinhude)

Carved horse from Borry near Hamlin, traces of paint, c. 1850. (Bomann Museum)

I n the eighteenth and nineteenth centuries the production of wooden toys in eastern and southern Germany was concentrated in Sonneberg, Berchtesgaden, Oberammergau and Seiffen. Oberammergau, famous for its staging of the celebrated passion play, produced religious carvings of all kinds – crucifixes, animals and figures for Christmas cribs and Noah's Arks.

In Berchtesgaden in 1860, 400 families were engaged in woodworking, 170 craftsmen specialised in the production of sets of painted wooden chip boxes, there were 120 turners, and 60 wood carvers. In 1909, George Zimmerman opened an art school and a museum where one can see the prototypes of articles which are still in production.

In the Erzgebirge mountains on the borders of Czechoslovakia, the town of Seiffen perfected a system for mass-producing small animals for farms and Noah's Arks. This was done by shaping circular wooden discs in such a way that when the discs were sliced through like a cake, each section formed an animal shape that only needed painting, and perhaps ears and horns added. In 1900 nearly 1,400 people made a living from making these zoo and farm yard animals, as well as Christmas cribs.

Board-sided wooden horse with leather seat, made in Schleswig-Holstein, c. 1860. (Hamburg Altonaer Museum)

Sonneberg, in the heart of the Thuringian forest, and the surrounding villages and small towns had made turned wooden household goods and small toys since the seventeenth century. Before the advent of a railway network, these products were carried down the mountains on the backs of pedlars or collected by horse and cart and taken to the great annual fairs which were held in Nuremberg, Dresden, Erfurt and Leipzig. Towards the end of the nineteenth century larger wooden items were produced in Thuringia.

In 1870, the year before Bismark became the first Chancellor of a united German Reich, Freidrich Heyn opened a carving factory at Neustadt for the production of horses and animals for merry-go-rounds. In his book *Fairground Art*, Geoff Weedon lists half a dozen other firms in the region of Sonneberg which were making carousel figures at the turn of the century.

A carved and painted prancing horse in the Bomann museum, Celle, and the entwined rocking sea-monsters in the Germanisches National Museum in Nuremburg are perhaps evidence that these carousel makers (such as Freidrich Heyn or Carl Müller) also made rocking horses for children's nurseries.

Ohrdruf, a village south of Gotha on the river Ohra was the home to many factories making toys, buttons and porcelain. In 1905 a magazine article stated that 100,000 horses a year were made there. It went on to describe one particular factory whose output was 30,000 a year. The machinery was powered by water and steam and used great stacks of fir, poplar and beech logs which were piled up outside.

The inner frame of the horse was a simple wooden structure covered with padding. The legs were cut-out by special carving machines. Large planks of wood were steamed and bent into shape, dried out in special heated rooms, and then sliced up into six parallel strips to make the rockers. The horse heads were made in moulds from glue and layers of wet cardboard; when dry the two halves were clamped together and finished by hand then fixed to the frame which was covered with canvas and stuffed with straw clippings. The horse was then covered with a plush-like material or, in the case of the more expensive models, with calf or pony skin. Ears, mane and tail of horsehair were then affixed and the final touches of paint to eyes, nostrils and hoofs applied. Packed in large wooden crates with their rockers and wheeled platforms the horses were dispatched to the port of Hamburg and exported to all parts of the world until the outbreak of the First World War which brought the thriving industry to a halt.

After the war and the following years of austerity, the toy industry in Thuringia and Erzgebirge recovered so that by 1929 the German toy trade journal, the *Deutsche Spielwaren Zeitung*, listed over a dozen firms dealing in wooden horses.

In West Germany, another centre for wooden toys specialized in making horses for the cheapest end of the toy trade. The Odenwald horses had simple rounded barrel shaped bodies and straight little legs standing upright on wheeled platforms and occasionally fixed to bow rockers.

A recent article in the magazine section of the *Darmstadt Echo* for 16 December 1989 on the past history of the Odenwald toy trade is illustrated with a photograph taken in 1907 of Adam Guyot and his assistant Martin solemnly sitting in their best Sunday clothes surrounded by a workshop full of toy horses. Another local paper, also published in December 1989, prints under the caption 'Last of a Long Line', a recent photograph of Adam Krämer in his workshop in Beerfurth putting the finishing touches to the batch of horses he has just made.

Adam Krämer took over the workshop from his father in 1961; the sizes and patterns of his horses are still those

Rocking sea dragons, carved in lime wood, nineteenth century. (Germanisches Nationalmuseum, Nuremberg)

Black-painted wooden horse, leather harness, horsehair mane and tail with iron support. Height: 38½in. (96cm). (Schloss Gottorf, Schleswig Holsteinsches Landesmuseum)

Two wooden horses by Adam Krämer, 1988. Height: 6in. (15cm). Length: approximately 4in. (10cm).

A wooden horse with horsehair mane and tail by Gudrun Becht, carved using tools which have been in his family for 150 years, 1991.

used by his grandfather in 1899 and are exactly like those turned out at the beginning of the century by Adam Guyot of Rohrback, and Fritz Beilstein and Frederick Glenk of Niederhausen. In those days nearly every house in the district contained a toy workshop. Times were hard. Families were large, the yield from their small holdings was insufficient to keep them fed all the year round even though the basic diet was soup and potatoes. Some tried to keep going by running small shops or fostering children but most spent long hours turning out quantities of cheap wooden toys many of which found their way into neighbouring Belgian and Luxembourg markets. The struggle to keep afloat is not so hard for Adam Krämer today. He repairs old rocking horses and makes a lot of tiny small-scale horses for sale in German museum shops.

*Wooden horse. Height: 25in.
(62.8cm). Length: 30in. (75cm).
(Detmold Lippisches
Landesmuseum)*

*Painted board-sided horse, 1930.
(Lubeck Museum für Kunst und
Kulturgeschichte)*

*Pine horse on underslung swing-
stand, Southern German twentieth
century. (Germanisches
Nationalmuseum Nuremberg)*

Head of a playground horse by Nagy Keistof, 1970s. (Kecskemet Museum, Hungary)

Fantasy horse by Nagy Keistof, 1970s. (Kecskemet Museum, Hungary)

The large market town of Kecskemet lies half-way between Budapest and the Yugoslav border. Its Folk Museum is a lovely place for children. Inside, on special days they are allowed to put on plastic aprons and splash about with water and coloured wodges of wool and learn how felt is made. On display is the finished article in the form of the great waterproof cloaks formerly worn by Hungarian horsemen rounding up their herds of wild horses. In the park outside during the summer months the visitors can wander into Mongolian circular yurts and other shelters made from felt, and admire a wide selection of felt rugs and pictures which are hung inside. In the children's playground is another special treat, stylised horses-and-coaches and single rocking horses designed by Nagy Keistof, a young sculptor whose imaginative work for children's playgrounds can be seen in Budapest and other Hungarian towns. Also on display in Kecskemet Museum are enlarged copies of old photographs showing scenes from village life a hundred years ago. In several can be seen little children playing with rustic home-made horses.

Once over the border into Yugoslavia one can find in a few small country towns local carpenters who make doors, window frames, rustic furniture and who occasionally produce simple rocking horses. In Belgrade, the Komisiona Galerija sells factory made rocking horses, covered in skin or plush on wooden rockers.

All Souls' Night in mid-winter and spring festivals are celebrated in Hungary, Poland, Bulgaria and Roumanian villages with boisterous processions. Drums are beaten, horns are blown, devil masks and shaggy head-dresses are worn, a lot of rough play often involves dancing around and riding on hobby-horses. These noisy peasant festivities are thought perhaps to have their roots in Ancient Greece. There are references to hobby-horses in classical Greek and Roman literature.

Nearly two and a half thousand years ago Alcibiades the vainglorious young general of the Peloponnesian War went to consult Socrates on the impending and ill-fated naval expedition to Sicily and found the old gentleman riding a hobby-horse at play with his children. In more recent times, until about thirty years ago village children in Greece had only home-made toys to play with, and sticks they rode would more often have donkey heads than horse heads.

Today Barbie and her Greek sister 'Bibi-Bo' doll, have taken the place of the rag dolls little girls used to make for themselves. The influx of foreign capital since 1970 has led to the creation of plastics firms and factories mass-producing toys. Half a dozen enterprises now advertise stuffed plush horses on metal frames and rockers. Only the firm of Laro, who specialize in nursery furniture, makes a simple wooden rocking horse.

ABOVE AND LEFT
A playground horse and ram by Nagy Keistof, Budapest.

Village horse, Kecskemet Museum.

Carrying horses down the mountain. (Tiroler Volkskunst Museum)

Ortisei, Val Gardena.

RIGHT AND FAR RIGHT
Making toys and horses in Val Gardena. (Altes Holzspielzeug aus Gröden, Rita Stäblein)

As the traffic races along the new elevated motorway which rises up the valley from Bolzano, over the Brenner Pass and down to Innsbruck, it is easy to flash past the exit sign, just before the Italian frontier, for 'Val Gardena'. Thirty years ago it was different. A long steep haul up the valley became even steeper once the main road was left behind. The farms and villages were widely scattered; the main town Ortesei, now a popular ski resort, was often cut off by avalanches and landslides.

This high isolated valley is known for two things. Firstly the strange language which all the older inhabitants still speak – 'Gerdena' or ladin which is not a dialect, but an archaic form of latin. The other particularity of the Val Gardena is that it is the place where up to 1914, millions of 'Dutch' dolls were made every year. During the long snowbound winter months nearly every household in the valley was employed carving whitewood toys and dolls, while a few master craftsmen turned out crucifixes, madonnas, infant Jesus and holy saints for catholic churches throughout the world. These artefacts were collected by some of the richer local families, stored in their barns ready packed-up and, before the railway was built, carried down the mountains to the great spring fair in Nuremberg.

One of these families was that of Adolf Sevoner, who now runs the firm of Sevi.

"Our firm Sevi was founded by my great-grandfather in 1831. Now my son (the fifth generation) is running the firm. Rocking horses were made and sent all over Europe by my three ancestors. They were entirely handcarved in wood and handpainted. In 'Val de Gherdeina' (ladin), 'Val Gardena' (Italian), 'Gröden' (German), the whole production used to be made by cottage workers. Each family was specialized in making just one article, sometimes in different sizes. Rocking horses were made in different sizes. There were two types of rocking horses; in our language, the 'Ciaval da Cuna' (cradle) the 'Ciaval da Nanieres' (seesaw).

"In our valley some ten thousand people speak 'Gherdeina' – ladin – a neo-latin language. In two nearby valleys a very similar language is spoken by another ten thousand people. All of us also speak German and Italian almost fluently.

"The last woodcarver who made rocking horses, and whom I knew very well, died some forty years ago. I am 75. But now nobody in the valley makes rocking horses, though my son has just created a new one which is going into production. Let us hope with good selling chances.

"Before the last war some five or six firms were producing or selling toys mostly made by cottage workers. Nowadays we are the only toy manufacturer in the valley. We employ fifty people plus a hundred cottage workers."

Another well-known name in the Val Gardena is the Moroder family. Today Robert Moroder runs the local museum in Ortisei. In 1980 Dr Edgar Moroder published a large illustrated book which traces the history of the family from the middle ages to the present day and charts how its network spread world-wide. In 1799, Josef Moroder (1760–1812) was installed in Valencia, Spain. By 1874 there was another little clan in Lyons, France, and in 1908 a USA branch in Milwaukee. A few years later representatives of the firm were in California, Argentina, Chile, Venezuela and South Africa. The Moroders specialized in carving large figures of saints and other religious statues. Their 1910 catalogue shows they also dealt in Dutch dolls and wooden toys. The Spanish connection would perhaps explain the manufacture of Dutch style dolls in Spain in the nineteenth century.

The other two families engaged in the export of goods from the Val Gardena were Insam (1820–1925) and Prinoth (1895). They merged before the end of the century and established agents in Nuremberg, Paris and London. Their 1888 catalogue shows plain wooden horses in several sizes and brightly painted toy rocking horses mounted with a variety of riders.

ABOVE Ortisei horse. Height: 17in. (43cm). Length: 16in. (40cm). (Pollock's Toy Museum)

ABOVE LEFT Two Ortisei horses, 1918. Height: 13in. and 14½in. (32 and 36cm). (Altes Holzspielzeug aus Gröden, *Rita Stäblein*)

A page from the sample book of Insam and Prinoth, 1888. (Altes Holzspielzeug aus Gröden, Rita Stäblein)

Push-along Beech horse from Ortisei, 1912. (Pollock's Toy Museum)

After the First World War the map of the Tyrol was redrawn and the Val Gardena ceased to be part of the Austro-Hungarian Empire. The firm Insam and Prinoth passed into the hands of a charming young girl who, after her marriage to an officer in the Italian Air Force, went off to live in Bolzano. The factory was sold, the remaining stock was piled up in a barn and the family house was only occupied during the summer holidays. In 1960 the contents of the barn, dutch dolls, horses, toys still wrapped up in their pre-1914 brown paper parcels were bought by Pollock's Toy Museum and transported to another barn in Kent, England.

It could be argued that the toys from Val Gardena should have been labelled made in Austria and that only the papier mâché horses made near Mantua down in the plain of Lombardy should be classified as Italian. In July 1916 the trade magazine *Games and Toys* reported that a large number of these Italian horses were being imported into England by the Italian Products Agency. Over a hundred different patterns were available. The horses were extremely light yet in spite of this, were strong and durable. Until recently papier mâché horses were also made in

Sicily, along with masks and other carnival novelties.

Today, in addition to the new 'Sevi' wooden horse, the firm T T Toys makes a range of fluffy rocking animals and Peg Perego Pines of Milan, famous for its very modern pedal cars and motor bikes, produce 'Rocky', a large coin-in-the-slot rocking horse seen in shopping arcades.

In his important book on the history of toys in Spain, Matheos José Corredor reveals the existence in the royal palace in Aranjuez of a large wooden rocking horse very similar to the cavalry horse made for Charles XII of Sweden and now in the library of Kavlas Castle. Another illustration shows a strange little spotted horse designed by Joseph Mario Gorris, circa 1930 and now in the large toy collection of Doña Maria Antonia Pelouzy.

Papier mâché horses were made in Seville, Valencia, Barcelona and Zaragoza by the same firms which made masks and large heads for religious processions. In a country where most children play at bull fighting there were also papier mâché bulls to ride, and nowadays a variety of coin-in-the-slot bulls are made by the plastic firms of Falgas in Figueras not far from Barcelona and Plasticos Mayalke of Alicante.

Papier mâché horse, Italian Products Agency. Games and Toys, July 1916.

Head of papier mâché horse, twentieth century. (El Juquete en España)

Papier mâché horse, twentieth century. (El Juquete en España)

Papier mâché bull designed by Joseph Maria Gollis. (El Juquete en España)

20

Perhaps Marxist political theories have encouraged the study of peasant cultures and the collection of Folk Art in eastern European countries after the Second World War. In Poland, the Ethnographical Museums in Warsaw, Cracow and other large Polish towns have a great number of wooden horses of all types. The collections are well documented, the provenance, the dates and the names of the makers are well known. In Warsaw for example, in the State Ethnographical Museum there are about five hundred folk toys, most of them horses of one kind or another. The curator Teresa Lewinska writes:

"There are horses with wagonettes, horses on wheels, horses with riders, moving horses on sticks, horses to be pulled. The collection can be divided into two categories:

a horses made at home by grandfathers, fathers, elder brothers and sisters for the sole use of the family.
b horses produced in the South of Poland in the traditional centres of toy production in the Kielce, Rzeszów, Zywiec, and Myslenice centres.

"The horses from each centre made by traditional techniques and simple tools are different in shape, ornamentation and colouring.

"In each centre, toys are made in a few villages and in each village there are a few families dealing with toy-production. Each village is specialized in some kinds of toys. It is known that the most beautiful horses may be bought in one village while in another one the most beautiful cradles for dolls or toys on sticks for the youngest children. Each toy workshop is a small factory where the whole family is employed. Father prepares the work, choosing the right material and cutting out all the parts of the toy. His son puts the parts together and his wife paints the toy and decorates it. Women usually sell toys at the fairs, markets and church fairs.

"Folk toys are still very popular with local people. Tradition plays an important role here. There was a custom that parents coming back from the fair should bring these kind of toys to their children. The other thing is that folk toys are made of wood and being colourful are attractive to the children."

Home-made horse, before 1939, for unknown family. Length: 27½in. (70cm). Height: 19in. (48cm). (Warsaw Ethnographical Museum)

LEFT Horse made by the folk sculptor Martan Brudek (1895–1981) in Bogoria, for his grandchildren. Painted in red, pink rockers. Rabbitskin mane, horse hair mane, string harness, 1955. (Okregowe Museum Sandomierzu)

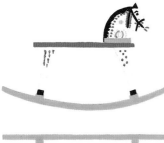

Drawings for a painted wooden horse by Tadeusz Rakowski, 1988.

The craftsmen who make these Polish toys can either sell them in street markets on their own account, or through co-operatives in Southern Poland. The 'Milenium' Co-operative, 28 S W Tomasza Street, Cracow, distributes the toys throughout Poland and deals with exports. In Warsaw, Cepelia (Central Union of Folk and Artistic Handicrafts) has a similar function. In Gostyn, there is a factory which since 1956 has produced various kinds of horses, for home sales and export. Their address is, Spoldzielnia Pracy 'Pallas', ul.Nowe Wrota 7, 63-800 Gostyn.

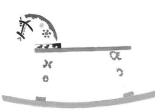

Drawings for a painted wooden horse by Stanislas Giszelc, 1989. (Lodz Ethnographical Museum)

Rocking seat made by Stanislaw Narog, 1985. Length: 62½in. (16cm). Height: 4½in. (11.5cm). (Warsaw Ethnographical Museum)

Rocking chair made by Stanislaw Narog, 1987. Length: 14in. (36cm). Height: 11in. (28cm). (Warsaw Ethnographical Museum)

Horse made by Jozef Cekala, for his children, 1950. Length: 38¼in. (97cm). Height: 21½in. (55cm). (Warsaw Ethnographical Museum)

Made by Teofil Szczygiel in the village of Lackowice. Painted blue and white. (Zywiec Museum)

RUSSIA

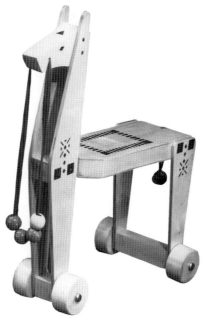

Not far from the ancient city of Novogorod, surrounded by the dense forests and situated between the Volga and the Uzal river, is the town of Gorodets. It is famous for its painted wooden ware. The peasant craftsmen used local birch and lime woods, as well as dark water-stained oak which they retrieved from stray logs which came adrift from the rafts of timber which in the past were floated down the river. They made distaffs for spinning, simple benches and cupboards, sleighs and great quantities of kitchen utensils, bowls, plates, spoons and cups, all decorated with garlands of bright apple-like flowers, fantastic birds and spirited black horses painted directly onto the pale natural wood.

The plain backgrounds distinguish Gorodets ware from that of the neighbouring town of Kholhloma where ancient Russian techniques of icon painting are used to transform humble wooden plates and bowls into brilliant golden vessels. The golden background was achieved by first coating the plain wood with a thin solution of clay, then applying a little linseed oil, followed by powdered tin. Next the design was painted on in black and cinnabar red and finally, before drying off in an oven, several coatings of varnish made from flaxseed oil were applied.

From medieval times these village craftsmen took their wares to be sold at the great fairs which were held outside the monasteries of Novogorod. Today it is the nearby town of Semyonev which has become the centre for

Gelman Daya Horoshabin who died in her youth in Moscow, 1900.

the export trade of this traditional Russian wooden ware. Toys such as rocking horses, necklaces, cannisters and other novelties have been added. The tiny co-operatives of local craftsmen set up after the Russian Revolution have expanded, over a thousand people are employed to work in large factories and graduate art students are trained in new methods of keeping alive an ancient craft. In nearby Zagorsk, the Toy Museum helps to further these aims. The Toy Museum was founded in Moscow in 1918 by the painter and art critic Nikolai Dmitrivich Bartram. As its full title The Art Education Museum of the USSR Academy of Pedagogical Sciences implies it was hoped that the museum would not only collect and exhibit Soviet toys, but would also be a centre for many other activities connected with the design and manufacture of toys. These aims gained in importance when the museum moved to the toy making centre of Zagorsk in 1931.

At present the museum collection numbers over thirty thousand exhibits. In addition to the traditional brightly painted Folk toys which have come from all parts of the Soviet Union, there are toys from archaeological digs, portraits of children dating from the 18th century, children's furniture and toys which came from nationalised country mansions and former royal palaces. Now tucked away in a museum storeroom is one of these grander toys, a large rocking horse made in the 18th century for the tzarina's little sons.

Vladimir Horoshabin on his horse, early twentieth century.

Painted wooden horse from Gorodets.

Papier mâché wheeled horse designed by N P Lavroy, 1930. (Zagorsk Toy Museum)

Papier mâché horse from the Moscow area, nineteenth century. (Zagorsk Toy Museum)

Patricia Mullins has dealt extensively with Sweden in her book and I am not discussing that country further. However, I have gleaned some additional information on horses from Denmark, Norway and Finland.

Legoland in Billund, Denmark is a great tourist attraction. In addition to the Lego Village, it has a large collection of dolls and toys, but no rocking horses. Kirsten Marten Stadelhofer, writes:

(In the nineteenth century) "Rocking horses in Denmark were luxury toys only bought by well-to-do families, not from toyshops, but from saddlers such as J J Lund in Copenhagen. They were also made in prison workshops. In the book *Det Legede VI Med*, by Jens Sigsquard and Ib Varmild, an old rocking horse is referred to. It came from 'Svendstrup' a manor house on the island of Zeeland. It lived in a corridor on the first floor and when the grandchildren came to visit their grandmother, it was considered a great honour to be given permission to ride it. This horse is now in the Danish Folk Museum in Brede, Lyngby, which also houses a large oak horse on cradle rockers, from Amager, dated 1778. Among the other ten horses in the collection is a more recent one designed in Copenhagen some 40 years ago by Kay Bøjesen."

Board-sided oak horse with touches of paint. From Amager, 1778. Length: 50in. (127cm). Height: 28¼in. (72cm). (Dansk Folkemuseum)

Pinewood horse, white and black paint, leaves and flowers on the rockers. Formerly from a Manor House, Svendstrup, 1896. Length: 62in. (157cm). Height: 40in. (112cm). (Dansk Folkemuseum)

*FAR RIGHT Kay Bøjesen
lacquered rocking horse. Designed
1950s, still in production in 1980s.
Height: 10¼in. (26cm) to 12½in.
(32cm).*

*A well-worn wooden horse,
c. 1910–20. (Roskilde Museum,
Denmark)*

*Three horses made by Norwegian
prisoners. c. 1860. (Norsk
Folkemuseum, Norway)*

*Rocking seat 'Lotte', Brabrand,
Denmark, 1975 to 1990.
(K E Mathiasen)*

Kay Bøjesen (1886–1958) was one of Denmark's fore-most modern designers. He trained as a silversmith but also worked in steel, wood and other materials, designing a wide range of simple, useful objects which could be mass-produced by modern industrial methods. The toy soldiers, monkeys, bears, elephants and other animals made from oak or maple woods are full of humour and originality. The lacquered horses are 26 and 32cm high and are still in production.

In Norway, many rocking horses were imported from the Swedish firm Gemla or from England. From the middle of the last century a few horses were produced in Norwegian workshops or made to order for sale in saddlers' shops. Husfliden, a craft workers co-operative founded in 1891 and which still exists, also advertised rocking sheep which were popular with Norwegian children.

Finland has a small toy making industry producing most of the standard educational nursery toys in plain wood or painted brightly. Two firms make rocking horses. The 'Jukka' horses are made by the Juho Jussila Company, who for the past 40 years have made simple birch wood horses either painted or left natural. They come in two sizes, 26cm or 65cm. Paulina and Kaija Aarikka are both talented designers creating simple, modern wooden candlesticks, bowls, Christmas tree ornaments and toys, notably a flock of amusing carved sheep. Since 1984 their catalogue has featured a basic barrel-shaped, wooden rock-ing horse, 'Keinahoben'. Four years later a still more rudimentary horse was added called 'Poni'; both horses are 47cm high.

At the beginning of this century the firm of Fahrni and Co. was running an up-to-date factory and making a wide range of wooden toys including rocking horses on cradle and bow rockers. In 1910 they started making horses from a new mixture of papier mâché which they had invented which was very strong and hard wearing. They were then covered with hide.

A catalogue now in the possession of the Folk Museum in Basle illustrates the products of another Swiss woodworking firm, Gebruder Strehler in Wald. The illustrations show wheeled platform horses on rockers and a variety of horses rearing on their hind legs like horses in a Spanish riding school. They are supported in their middle by several ingenious wooden devices.

In the April 1976 issue of *Heimatwerk*, an arts and crafts magazine, are the plans for a DIY rocking horse seat that can be assembled at home. This is a forerunner of a present day DIY horse project run by Rudolf Würgler from an old village school not far from Bern, half way between Frutigen and Adelboden.

Rudolf Würgler trained as an engineer. One day when he was restoring an old rocking horse he had found in the attic of his sister's house, he decided to make a more modern horse which could be packed flat and assembled with only four screws. The project got underway in 1986. Today the horse is produced in very small sizes for toys or ornaments, a child size, and a very large two metre size for grown-ups. These can be bought in plain wood or painted.

The originality of Rudolf Würgler's 'Ruedi-Rössli' horses lies in their painting. Würgler has organised a network of artists to do the work so that every horse is different; some are covered with trails of leaves and flowers, some are jigsaws of blue and green, some are red patterned in gold, some are in shades of pink and green. All are signed and no two are ever alike. Würgler says: "The artists have to accept my horses and I their style. We must know and appreciate each other to be able to work together. In order to have delivery in sensible quantities, I want as many collaborators as possible."

Illustration of horse made by Fahrni, in Rothrist, 1910. (Baden archives, Kinder Museum)

Cover of Gebr. Strehler catalogue, c. 1930. (Swiss Folk Museum, Basel archives)

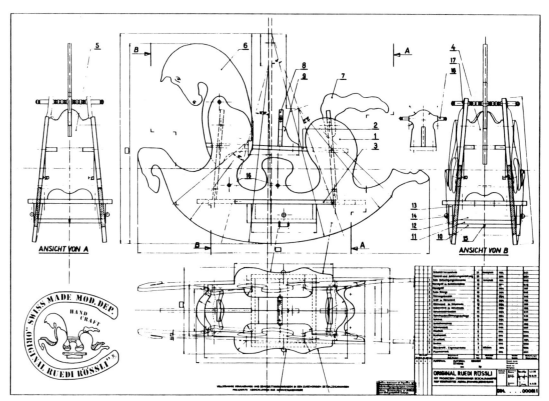

Plans for Rudolf Würgler's 'Ruedi-Rössli' horse.

This horse was probably the same as the DIY horse discussed in the craft magazine Heimetwerk, published in Zurich, March 1976.

ABOVE LEFT *Original 'Ruedi-Rössli', designed by Rudolf Würgler, hand-painted and available in several sizes, the smallest 8in. (20.5cm) long, the largest 237in (6 metres) long.*

Wooden horse, twentieth century. (Basel Historisches Museum)

ABOVE RIGHT *Horse on cradle rockers, c. 1930. (Baden Kinder Museum)*

Canada

During the last hundred years many American and British Firms have exported toys and rocking horses to Canada. These were sold through mail order catalogues, or in shops in large towns. As these imported horses have been adequately covered in the main volume, they are not discussed here. However many provincial Canadian museums have in their collection horses which were locally made in small country workshops or by devoted fathers for their own children. It is these horses which have been rounded up and illustrated in the following pages.

The first horse made in Canada is referred to in a series of bills and a receipt drawn up in Quebec in 1796. In January of that year, François Baillargé was then 37 years old. He was the son of a sculptor and had studied in Paris at the Royal Academy and was known for the work he had carried out in several Quebec churches. On 26 February 1796 the 'hoby hors' was delivered and on 5 March he received from Mr Gragy three guineas for the horse and a cradle. The final receipt dated 26 July states that the carving and painting of the horse on wheels was completed. The documents also confirm that the horse was not mounted on a platform, but that the legs were wide apart and fixed onto parallel bars to which the wheels were attached.

The horse carved by François Baillargé has not survived. It was in all probability a more sophisticated beast than the charming rustic animals now in the collections of the Canadian Museum of Civilization in Hull and other provincial museums. Characteristically they had simplified little heads, solid pregnant bodies and broomstick legs mounted on crude home-made platforms or rockers. Little is known of these early Canadian toys, beyond the region where they were found and sometimes the name of a family to whom they had belonged on the label: Joseph Boucheau, Les Eboulements, Chevalier family, Très Saint-Redempteur, Gagnon family, Cap-au Corbeau, Amedée Seguin, carpenter in Riquad. Looking at these home-made horses one thinks of those early settlers, striving bravely to make a home in the wilderness with the simplest of tools, fashioning out of the forest which surrounded them most of the farm and household implements they needed.

In the Canadian Museum of Civilization and also in the Glenbow Museum in Calgary, Alberta, are some strange primitive horses roughly shaped by the carpenters of several Hutterite communities. Founded in the early sixteenth century in Moravia (Czechoslovakia) by Jacob Hutter, the Hutterites are a strict anabaptist sect, who to escape persecution fled to Hungary, then Rumania and Russia, and, finally, like the Amish and other Mennonite religious sects found sanctuary, and even prosperity in the farming communities they established in Alberta, Manitoba and Saskatchewan in the New World.

LEFT *Rocking chair, painted red with traces of harness. From St. Michel de Bellechasse, Quebec. (National Museums of Canada)*

FAR LEFT *Oak horse, painted black, blue leather harness, glass bead eyes, horse hair tail. Made by Rosaire Leblanc – Ste Sophie de Levrard, Quebec. (National Museums of Canada)*

Horse made in 1969 by George M. Stahl for his son from various woods, while helping build a hutterite colony, near Huxley, Alberta. Height: 26in. (65cm). Length: 38½in. (96.5cm). (Glenbow Museum)

ABOVE RIGHT *'Walking' rocking horse from Saint John, New Brunswick. (National Museums of Canada)*

RIGHT *Shoofly, Height: 21in. (52cm). Length: 36in. (90cm). (National Museums of Canada)*

William Lyon Mackenzie King aged two, in 1878. Canada's future tenth Prime Minister, riding possibly a Moritz Lindner horse. (Woodside National Historic Site)

RIGHT *Rocking horse made by carpenter on the estate of Robert Stewart at Strathgartney in Bonshaw. (Prince Edward Island Museum)*

A horse in the Prince Edward Island Museum bears witness to another more romantic personal dream that, over a hundred years ago, found fulfilment in the Canadian wilderness. Leaving his staid and respectable home in Great Russell Street London, Robert Bruce Stewart set off for Canada to create for himself a life worthy of his Scottish Jacobite ancestors. In 1863, by the age of 50, he had achieved his goal, 'Strathgartney', a large estate overlooking the Northumberland Strait, on Prince Edward Island. There he had built a splendid mansion, handsomely furnished with fine pictures and books. There he presided over his family of nine children, his retinue of servants, with even a highland piper to grace his meals. The ingenious horse now housed in the museum was made for the children by the estate carpenter.

By the end of the nineteenth century and the beginning of the twentieth comfortably off families could obtain all the necessities and luxuries they desired from either the Hudson Bay Company's or Eaton's mail order catalogues. A few copies of these early catalogues have survived in the Ontario and the Manitoba State Archives but the shooflies and rocking horses illustrated would all seem to be American imports either from Morton E Converse or the Whitney Reed Chair Company. Other toy imports came from Great Britain, and although at one time Lines Brothers had a factory in Canada, rocking horses were not made there but shipped out from the English factory.

Janet Holmes of the Royal Ontario Museum, in the entry 'Toys and Games', which she wrote for the *Canadian*

Encyclopaedia mentions several firms who made wooden toys: The Toronto firm of C T Brandon & Co. (1890), the Gendron Manufacturing Co. (1890–1970) and Edouard Alfred Martineau of Montreal (1876–1914). The only firm however which specialised in all types of wooden horses was the firm Moritz Lindner of Berlin (now called Kitchener), in Ontario.

Moritz Eduard Lindner was born in Germany, in Waldenburg, Saxony, in 1816. In 1856 he emigrated with his wife and little son to Canada. After 11 years trying to make his way in a variety of odd jobs he moved to Berlin, Ontario, which had a large German community and opened a shop where he sold toys he had made himself. This business was successful making sleighs, baby carriages, rocking horses and other kinds of horses.

In the early 1970s, an elderly lady, Miss Irmgard Bitzer, a granddaughter of Moritz Lindner, gave to the Doon Heritage Pioneer Village not only the rocking horses made by her grandfather which were stored, in mint condition, in the attic of her house, but also a large collection of photographs, newspaper clippings, account books and other valuable documentation. In 1976, Alfred J K Scheak compiled a 50-page research study of the Lindner collection and subsequently the present Curator, Thomas Reitz, published in the November 1990 edition of the *Waterloo County Times* an interesting article, part of which, with his permission, is quoted here:

"Rocking horses were made in Berlin, now Kitchener, by Moritz Lindner's toy manufactory, later known as the 'Berlin Life-Size Display Horse Works'. By the 1890s, the firm had moved into the manufacture of life-size horses on which a harness was displayed (a surviving example is on exhibit in the Harness Shop at Doon Heritage Crossroads), and the toy line appears to have become secondary.

"During the 1880s, Lindner's output included: velocipede horses, horses on wheels, horses and carts, double horses, rocking horses and chair horses. Twenty-nine different models were offered for sale, the different models varying in size. In a twelve-month period, during 1884 and 1885, a total of 2,165 horse-related toys were sold by Lindner, accounting for 44% of his total output for the period. And during the months before Christmas, sales of horse-related toys far exceeded sales of buggies and carts and doll carriages.

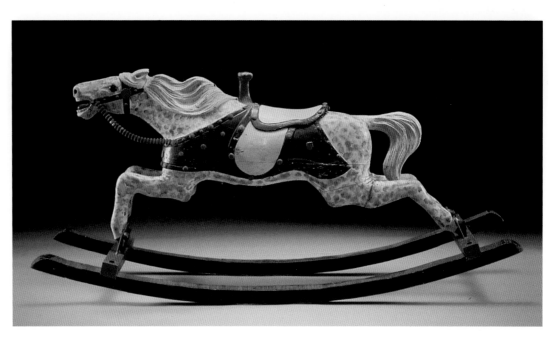

"Lindner wholesaled his product line to 'house furnishing, woodenware and fancy good dealers' throughout Ontario and Quebec, although somewhat surprisingly, his account books list few sales to local Waterloo County stores. Sales were made, however, to Steubing and Smith, a Berlin wholesaler of 'fancy goods', perhaps indicating that local sales were made through a middleman.

Carousel horse on rockers. From Halifax, Nova Scotia. (National Museums of Canada)

Head of horse by Moritz Lindner, c. 1870 (Doon Heritage)

Moritz Lindner, c. 1885. (Doon Heritage)

31

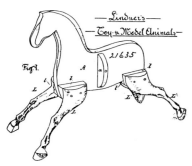

Moritz Lindner's receipt dated 1885 and patent application. (Doon Heritage)

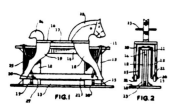

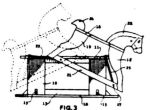

Drawings for Olson patent.

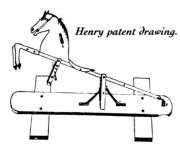

Henry patent drawing.

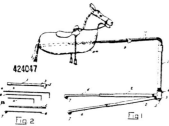

Fleury patent drawing.

Masch patent drawing.

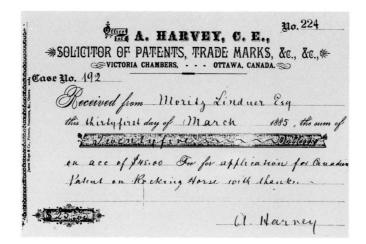

"In 1885 Lindner received a Canadian patent for 'toy and model horses', this same patent was registered in the United States in 1889. The patent specifications give us a view as to how rocking horses were made and the improvements Lindner introduced in their construction:

'My invention relates to the construction and manufacture of imitation animals, such as rocking horses and toys used for riding either with or without rockers or wheels.'

'The better class of these toys and model animals have hitherto, when strength was required, been cut out of solid timber, and consequently been both very heavy and expensive, while it was difficult to shape them true to nature. To produce a rocking horse out of solid timber requires a piece of wood very large and heavy compared with the size of the finished article, and the weight of the same is a source of expense in transport and of danger in the hands of children when playing with them.

'My improvements overcome these objections; and they consist, mainly, in constructing merely a flat wooden skeleton and to covering it with a moulded shell or skin consisting of a number of layers of stiffened canvas or other similar material formed and moulded in two halves upon a more or less perfectly-shaped model, the legs (or other slender portions of an animal requiring strength or stiffness) being cut out of solid wood and fastened to the skeleton thus producing substantially a hollow article.'"

Born of Norwegian parents, Clifford Olson grew up on the family farm outside Porcupine Plain, Saskatchewan. At one time he drove a school bus and worked in a hardware store. Like all the members of his family he was engaged in the work of the Reorganised Church of Jesus Christ of Latter Day Saints, and the welfare of Senior Citizens and the mentally handicapped. He is a man of

many hobbies and an inventive turn of mind. He is known locally for the large fibreglass moving animals he created which are in demand for school functions, parades and carnivals. He also had a wry sense of humour, as for example in the height of summer adorning the eaves of his house with festoons of plastic icicles.

In 1960 Clifford Olson together with his brothers Ivan and Merlin took out a Canadian patent for a rocking horse, which they manufactured until 1977. The horse is still made and sold for the benefit of the handicapped by the Porcupine Opportunities Program, Box 697, Porcupine Plain, Saskatchewan.

CANADIAN PATENTS

The Canadian Patent Office lists a great number of patents for rocking horses, nearly all however are extensions of American patents. A few relate to original Canadian inventions.

1885, Canadian Patents 21635–294947–412109
LINDNER, MORITZ
Berlin, Ontario
Rocking horse and other toys, with or without rockers or wheels, or models used for harness-makers and others, consisting of a flat wooden skeleton cover with a moulded skin consisting of a number of layers of stiffened canvas, or other similar material and joined in two halves. The legs being cut out of solid wood.

1922, British Patent 183.952
CHAPDELAINE, N. & INTERNATIONAL TOY CO.
2 Place d'Armes, Montreal
Horse on wheels, that can be propelled by shifting the weight of the rider.

1928, Canadian Patent 280.857.
EASON, VICTOR ALBERT
Toronto, Ontario
A rocking horse in a supporting frame and held by tension springs in an unstable position. Balance of the horse maintained by compensating for variation in weight of user, by means of a horizontal line of holes in the base in which a pivot may be selectively fitted.

1936, Canadian Patent 375.719.
HENRY, WILLIAM JAMES
Toronto, Ontario
A rocking horse consisting of an upright secured to a base. A bar with horses head one end and a spring at the other end.

1944, Canadian Patent 424.047.
FLEURY, ANDREW JOSEPH
Turner Valley, Alberta
A rocking horse comprising a cantilevered spring supporting a ridable model at its free end and supported on an upright standard at its opposite end.

1960, Canadian Patent 594.835.
MASCH, HELMUT
Hamilton, Ontario
A rocking horse mounted on a supporting frame and a complicated device of pins and rods on the stirrups.

Wooden horse, rope mane and tail, leather ears, drawing pin eyes, bolted to red rockers. (McCord Museum of Canadian History)

Shoofly belonging to a child who died in 1913, aged three. Painted white, red and black. Length: 35½in. (93cm). Height: 18½in. (47cm). (Manitoba Museum of Man and Nature)

ABOVE LEFT *Moritz Lindner display horse, c. 1890. (Doon Heritage)*

ABOVE RIGHT *Pinewood horse, carved from a single block, painted brown, light brown horsehair mane. Length: 17½in. (44cm). Height: 10½in. (26.5cm). (Musée de Vaudreuil-Soulanges)*

Children playing horses. Ming dynasty, porcelain paintings.

Horse lanterns, for Chinese New Year celebrations. Drawings by Chiang Yee from A Chinese Childhood, *1940.*

Riding Hobby Horses, 'The Hundred Children'. Scroll, Ming dynasty. (British Museum)

Children in many Far Eastern countries have played with hobby-horses since ancient times, or have dressed up as horses as part of the festivities on certain traditional holidays. A number of German or English rocking horses were imported into the region by well-to-do families and a few of these are illustrated in the main volume. In general, however, the region does not have a strong tradition of indigenous rocking horse manufacture as nurseries as we know them in Europe did not exist. However, the horse in its other forms was a popular toy.

Jaipur and Udaipur in Rajasthan, India are traditional centres for all kinds of animals made from papier mâché or cloth decorated with bits of paper and tinsel. Brightly lacquered wooden toys are also made. The horses are charming trifles, never large enough for a child to ride.

Rocking horses are also made in China, where they

are a twentieth century innovation. However hobby-horses made from bamboo have a long history in China. The first written account dates from the late Han dynasty (AD 25–220) and tells how a famous general was seen at the age of 14 riding around on a bamboo mount. In addition, porcelain from the Ming dynasty (1368–1644) has been found decorated with scenes of boys playing with hobby horses.

In the Department of Oriental Antiquities at the British Museum is a delicately painted hand-scroll, an eighteenth century copy of an earlier Ming painting entitled 'A Hundred Sons'. Six scenes from this scroll, depicting little boys riding hobby horses, playing with puppets, feeding a phoenix, saying their prayers, beating drums and dancing have been reproduced as postcards on sale in the museum.

In 1924 Chen Hegin (1892–1982) a specialist in children's education, designed a rocking horse for use in the Kindergarten he founded in Nanjing. Today most childrens' playgrounds are equipped with some kind of rocking toy made either by the big Beijing Education and Recreational Toy Factory or by other provincial toy factories. All the animals they produce have a cuteness reminiscent of Walt Disney characters.

Although there are no museums in China specifically for toys, there is however in Beijing an Association of Toys for Children run by Yi Zhi. The address is PO Box 155, 73 De Sheng Nien, Wai Street, Beijing, China.

The siege of Troy is not the only battle in which a decoy horse played its part. In Japan, legend has it that a thousand years ago or more, General Tamura-maro set out to relieve the Castle of Miharu, which was being attacked by tribes hostile to the Emperor. The journey was long and arduous and the Imperial Forces arrived in such a weakened state, that the battle went badly for them. Fortunately the General had packed in his baggage train one hundred saddled wooden horses which had been presented to him by the abbot of a Buddhist temple. The enemy was deceived, the Emperor's men were heartened and the tide of battle turned. Today at the Miharu shrine, a brisk trade in small brightly painted horses is carried on. The horses are not only souvenirs of a distant military

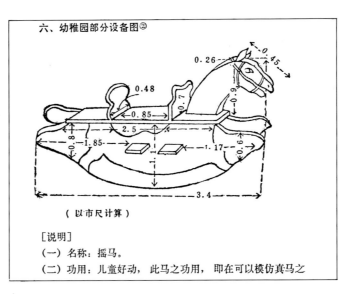

六、幼稚园部分设备图②

（以市尺计算）

［说明］

（一）名称：摇马。

（二）功用：儿童好动，此马之功用，即在可以模仿真马之

Chen Hegin, Chinese children's educationalist (1892–1982).

Drawing for horse designed by Chen Hegin, 1924.

FAR LEFT *Beijing Toy Factory horse, 1990.*

triumph, but charms to ward off disease and help children to grow up well and strong.

Like Chinese and European children, Japanese boys used to enjoy dressing up and playing at horses. At auction sales throughout Europe, Japanese business men are now buying porcelain dolls, teddy bears, tin toys and trains for private collections and Japanese museums. Recently, there has been a small but growing interest in rocking horses in Japan and quite a few English and Australian reproductions have been exported there over the past five years.

In Thailand and in the Philippines a large number of rocking horses and tricycle horses are being produced today. These are not indigenous products, but articles made for export, copied from originals supplied by foreign business men for sale in their home countries where they sometimes end up in unsuspecting 'antique' market stalls and shops.

Japanese Print, nineteenth century.

Horse made for export in Northern Thailand, 1990. Length: 39in. (99cm). Height: 23in. (58.5cm).

Old Horses at Rest

EUROPE

AUSTRIA

INNSBRUCK
Tiroler Volkskunst Museum (Folk Museum)

SALZBURG
Museum Carolina Augusteum

VIENNA
Museum der Stadt Wien

BELGIUM

BRUSSELS
Musée du Jouet

GHENT
The Ghent Folk Museum

MECHELEN
Speelgoed Museum

DENMARK

ARHUS
Kobstadmuseet 'Den Gamle By' (The Old Town Open Air Museum)

LYNGBY BREDE
Dansk Folkmuseum

MORS ISLAND
Glomstrup Manor

ROSKILDE
Roskilde Museum

FINLAND

HELSINKI
Doll & Toy Museum

FRANCE

MARCELLAZ ALBANAIS
L'Art de L'Enfance

NANTES
Musée de la Poupée et des Jouets Anciens

PARIS
Musée des Arts Décoratifs

POISSY
Musée du Jouet

STRASBOURG
Musée Alsacien

GERMANY

BERLIN
Berlin Museum

BRUNSWICK
Braunschweigisches Landesmuseum

CELLE
Bomann Museum

COBURG
Coburger Puppenmuseum

DETMOLD
Lippisches Landesmuseum

ERFURT
Thüringen Volkskundemuseum

ERLANGEN
Stadt Erlangen Museum

FRANKFURT
Historisches Museum

GIENGEN-an-der-Brenz
The Margarete Steiff Museum and Archives

GREFRATH
Kreis Viersen Museum

HAMBURG
Altonaer Museum

LUBECK
Museum Für Kunst und Kulturgeschichte

LUNEN
Museum der Stadt

MOLFSEE
Schleswig-Holsteinsches, Freilichtmuseum

MUNICH
Stadtmuseum

NUREMBERG
Germanisches National Museum
Museum Lydia Bayer

OBERAMMERGAU
Volkskundemuseum

OHRDRUF
Heimat Museum

ROTHENBERG
Spielzeug Museum

SCHLESWIG
Schloss Gottorf, Schleswig-Holsteinsches, Landes Museum
Stadtisches Museum

SONNEBERG
Spielzeug Museum

STEINHUDE
Spielzeug und Kinderwelt Museum

TECKLENBURG
Kreis Steinfurt Museum

GREAT BRITAIN

BANGOR
Penrhyn Castle

BATH
American Museum in Britain, Claverton Manor

BIRMINGHAM
Aston Hall

EDINBURGH
Museum of Childhood

HOVE
Hove Museum and Art Gallery

KING'S LYNN
Lynn Museum

LAYCOCK
Laycock Abbey

LONDON
Bethnal Green Museum of Childhood (V&A)
Museum of London, Barbican
Pollock's Toy Museum
Toy and Model Museum

MENAI BRIDGE
Museum of Childhood

MORPETH
Cambo House, Cambo

ROTTINGDEAN
The Grange Museum

THURSFORD
Cushing's Steam Museum

WELLS
Madam Tussaud's at Wookey Hole Caves

HUNGARY

KECSKEMET
Folk Museum

ITALY

ORTESEI
Val Gardena Museum

NETHERLANDS

DEN HELDER
Kathe Kreuse Poppen

DEVENTER
Gemeentemuseum Van Deventer

DOKKUM
Het Admiraliteitshuis

DORDRECHT
Gemeentemuseum Simon Van Gign

OOSTERHOUTY
Speelgoedmuseum

TONDEM
De Tooverlantaarn Speelgoedmuseum

NORWAY

OSLO
Norsk Folkmuseum

POLAND

CRACOW
Ethnographical Museum

LODZ
Archaeological and Ethnographical Museum

SANDOMIERZU
Museum Okregowe

WARSAW
State Ethnographical Museum

ZYWIEC
Museum Zywcu

RUSSIA

ZAGORSK
Toy Museum, USSR Academy of Pedagogical Sciences

SPAIN

BARCELONA
Museu d'Arts Industries i Tradicions Populeirs

FIGUERES
Museu del Joguet

SWEDEN

STOCKHOLM
Leksakmuseum
Nordiska Museet

SWITZERLAND

BADEN
Museum Für Kind und Spielzeug

BASLE
Historisches Museum Basel

BASEL
Museum Für Volkskunde

RIEHEN
Spielzeug und Dorfmuseum

USA

CHICAGO, Illinois
Historical Society

COLONIAL WILLIAMSBURG, Virginia
The Abby Aldrich Rockefeller Folk Art Centre

CONCORD, New Hampshire
New Hampshire Historical Society

DEERBORN, Michigan
Henry Ford Museum

DOYLESTOWN, Pennsylvania
Bucks County Historical Society

INDIANAPOLIS, Indiana
Children's Museum

KANSAS CITY, Kansas
The Toy and Miniature Museum

LANCASTER, Landis Valley, Pennsylvania
Pennsylvania State Farm Museum

NEW YORK
Museum of the City of New York
Historical Society

PHILADELPHIA, Pennsylvania
Museum of Art

ROCHESTER, New York
Margaret Woodbury Strong Museum

SALEM, Massachusetts
Essex Institute

SHELBURNE, Vermont
The Shelburne Museum

ST LOUIS, Missouri
The Eugene Field House Museum

STONY BROOK, New York
Museum at Stony Brook

WASHINGTON D.C.
D.A.R. Museum
The Washington Dolls' House and Toy Museum

WINCHENTON, Massachusetts
Historical Society

CANADA

CALGARY, Alberta
Glenbow Museum

CHARLOTTESTOWN, Prince Edward Island
Museum and Heritage Foundation

EDMONTON, Alberta
Provincial Museum

HALIFAX, Nova Scotia
Museum

HULL, Quebec
Canadian Museum of Civilisation

JORDAN, Ontario
Historical Museum of the Twenty

KINGSTON, Ontario
aclachlan Woodworking Museum

KITCHENER, Ontario
Doon Heritage Crossroads

LONDON, Ontario
Regional Art and Historical Museum

MONTREAL, Quebec
McCord Museum

NORTH YORK, Ontario
Black Creek Pioneer Village

SASKATOON, Saskatchewan
Western Development Museum

ST JOHN'S, Newfoundland
Historical Resources Division

STANSTEAD, Quebec
Historical Society

TORONTO, Ontario
Royal Ontario Museum

VANDREUIL-SOULANGES, Quebec
Musee Regional

WINNIPEG, Manitoba
Museum of Man and Nature

AUSTRALIA

GEELONG, Vic.
Barwon Grange

MELBOURNE, Vic
Como House,
'Rippon Lea'

PERTH, WA
Museum of Childhood

SYDNEY, NSW
Juniper Hall,
The Powerhouse Museum

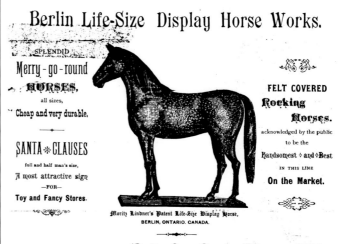

Advertisement for Berlin Life Size Display Horse Works. (Doon Heritage)

Index of Rocking Horse Manufacturers

This index does not claim to be comprehensive. It is a pooling of research by Marguerite Fawdry and Patricia Mullins. Some manufacturers whose names have been found in trade directories and journals were active only for a few years; others such as Lines Bros were active for many years. Significant manufacturers are described in detail in the main volume. The others are listed to help collectors who may have a one-off item produced by one of these smaller makers and to inspire them to further research. Where only one date is given it denotes a maker known to be active during that year but about whom further information is not currently available. Page numbers in brackets after certain manufacturers indicate that further information on them is contained in the main volume or the survey, the latter being indicated by the word 'Survey' before the page number.

AMERICA

Animal Manufacturing Co.
Carbondal, Illinois
1930

Arney Speciality Co.
State Street
Port Huron, Michigan
1909–15

Askam & Son
Philadelphia, Pennsylvania
1860

Barnes & Co.
Covington, Kentucky
1879

Benner Manufacturing Co.
Lancaster, Pennsylvania
1912

Bentley & Marqua
Cincinnati, Ohio
1878
See Marqua

Boylston, S & F
New York and
Rowayton, Connecticut
1867–90

Bradford Kingman
Boston
1856
(p. 222)

Brown, John H
449 West Street
New York
1866 Patent
(pp. 228–29)

Brown & Eggleston
New York
1856
(p. 222)

Bryant, John
San Francisco
c.1870
(p. 217)

Bushnell, E W
Philadelphia, Pennsylvania
1847–57
(p. 222)

Bushnell & Tull
Philadelphia, Pennsylvania
1857

Central Wheel & Manufacturing Co.
Sturgis, Michigan
1912

Christian, Andrew & Son
81 Maiden Lane, New York
1850–68
(pp. 216,229,246–51,265,275)

Christian & Dare
1868–80

Colby Bros
Waterbury, Vermont
1857

Colwell, Nicholas H,
see National Novelty Co.

Converse, Atherton D
see below

Converse, Morton E
Rindge, New Hampshire c. 1873
Winchendon, Massachusetts
1875–1931
(pp. 233,277–79)

Converse & Mason
1878–83

Converse, Morton E & Co
1883–1931
(pp. 277–79, 281)

Cororan Manufacturing Co.
Section Avenue & Foraker
Avenue
Norwood, Cincinatti, Ohio
1931–33

Cox, Gideon
335–37 High Street
Philadelphia, Pennsylvania
1825–1843
(p. 222)

Crandall, Benjamin Potter
Westerley, Rhode Island and
47 Courtlandt Street, New York
1840–70
(pp. 226,229,235,257,266–67)

Crandall, Benjamin Potter Jnr.
1840s–73s
(pp. 226,232,262–63)

Crandall, Charles Thompson
New York, NY
1850s–80s
(pp. 226,257–58)

Crandall, Jesse Amor
478 Broadway and later
Fulton Street, Brooklyn
New York
1850s–1906
(pp. 226, 231–33, 239, 244,
257–58, 261, 263–73, 275)

Crandall, William Edwin
New York, NY
1850s–90s
(pp. 226, 231–33, 257–58, 261,
263, 266, 268–69, 271–72)

Crandall & McKinstry
469 Grand
New York
1852

Dare, Charles W F
47 Courtlandt Street, New York
1867–1880s
(pp. 252–55)
See also Christian & Dare

Fisher, George
New York
1867–70

Fraley, G W
Philadelphia, Pennsylvania
1875

Gerrish, Woodbury C
14–16 Daniel Street
Portsmouth, New Hampshire
1840

Gibbs Toys
Canton, Ohio
1911

Goldstein, Charles & Victor
Jones Street, New York
1930

Hall Car Manufacturing Co.
Northville, Michigan
1906

Henderson & Co., E
New Hartford, Conneticut
1849–50

Hitchcock, M T
76 Sudbury Street
Boston, Massachusetts
1859
(pp. 226,239,258)

Hoffmire, Kelsey & Cornwell
65 Maiden Lane and
87–93 Mangin Street, New York
(p. 246)

Inter-State Manufacturing Co.
Port Huron, Michigan
1909

Janesville Products Co.
Dept 120, Janesville, Wisconsin
1919–41

Kingham
82 Lincoln Street
Boston, Massachusetts
1855
After 1855 Snow & Kingman

Kip Manufacturing Co.
Keene, New York
1875

Kirsch, Ernst
Pleasant Street
Amesbury, Massachusetts
1871 Patent
(pp. 231–32)

Long, William
Union Street
Philadelphia, Pennsylvania
1785–1833
(pp. 36,222)

Mace & Co., L H
East Houston Street, New York
1869–1911
(pp. 219, 235, 261, 278)

Mackenzie, P W & Smith, S W
1862 Patent
(pp. 226–28)

Marqua, P J
4th & Main Street
Cincinnati, Ohio
1860s-early 20th century

Later **Bentley & Marqua** and
Marqua and Stevens Carriage Toy
Co.
1910
(pp. 81, 83, 169, 226, 228, 232,
271, 274–76, 293)

Mecky, A
Philadelphia, Pennsylvania
1883

Meinecke & Son, Adolphe
Milwaukee, Wisconsin
1864–1929
(p. 215)

Metzler, Henry
1865 and 1868 Patents
(pp. 201,227–29)

Metzler & Cowperthwaite
New York
1867

National Novelty Co.
826–28 Broadway, New York
1904

Nichols, John
Baldwinsville
1878 Patent
(pp. 232,239–43)

Peabody, J A
1877 Patent
(pp. 232–33)

Peabody & Whitney
Boston, Massachusetts
1878
See Whitney Reed Chair Co.

Percival, L C
1865 Patent
(p. 228)

Pickering, Thomas
Portland, Connecticut
1875

Quigg, J F
Chicago, Illinois
1873

Reed Toy Co., W S
Leominster, Massachusetts
1875–97
Later Whitney Reed Chair Co.
(p. 281)

Reinhart, John
New York
1869 and 1873 Patents
(pp. 229,232–33,250)

Ross, Abbot Q
1878 Patent
(pp. 232,253)

Smith, Sandford Alvah
Smith Wood Products
Brattleboro, Vermont
1861–1912
From 1889 S A Smith & Co.
(p. 258)

Steinfeld Bros
620 Broadway, New York
1907
Sold shooflies

Stewart & Corbett
New York
1868–70

Tibbals, Lewis P
510 Broadway, New York
1860s and 1870s
(p. 266)

Travers, George W
New York
1880–90

Vanderbilt & McQueen
New York
1865

Vick, Alfred
1880 Patent
(pp. 232–33)

Washburn, Daniel T
New York
1867

Wentworth, J
Boston, Massachusetts
1868

Whitney, F A
Leominster, Massachusetts
1860

Whitney Reed Chair Co.
Leominster, Massachusetts
1897–1915
Previously W S Reed Toy Co.
(pp. 132, 169, 201, 229, 258, 276, 281–83)

Whitney Reed Corporation
1915–52
(pp. 283–87)

Woodworth, Arad & Daniel
Boston
1859 Patent
(pp. 226,239,258)

Yaggy & Kinley
Chicago, Illinois
1886–87

Yost, J A
214 Dock Street and
3rd Street & Girard Avenue
Philadelphia, Pennsylvania
1860–90

AUSTRALIA

Andrysik, Antonin
Brunswick and North Melbourne
1954–56
(p. 343)
See also Pamir

Aylward, James P
Thornbury, Melbourne
and later
Rutherglen, Victoria
1920s–58
(p. 338)

Bartlett, R J
77 St David Street, Fitzroy
1913–16
302 Gore Street
1916–20
41 Fenwick Street
Clifton Hill
1920–53
(pp. 49, 55–6, 258, 292, 294, 312–28, 331–323)

Bartlett, J R & A M
32a Abbott Grove, Clifton Hill
1953–63
480 Lower Plenty Road, Rosanna
1964–74
(pp. 328–30,333–35)

Benson Trading Co.
Melbourne
1969–1970s

Cyclops Lines
1950s–72
(pp. 305–7)
Owned by Lines Bros Ltd

Cyclops Toys
William Street, Leichardt, Sydney
1913–72
Melbourne
1972–present day
(pp. 304–5)

Hockley, Cess
Dubbo
New South Wales
(p. 340)

Hojak, Edward
Brunswick and late Doncaster,
Melbourne
1957–83
(pp. 340,344–47)

Pamir
Hawthorn, Melbourne
1956–59
(pp. 343–44)

Peets, Lou
Market Street
Toowong, Brisbane
c.1910–1966
(pp. 294,336–37)

Roebuck, Frederick
Newtown, Sydney
1885–90s
(pp. 290, 294, 298)
George Street, Sydney
1900–08
(pp. 293, 298)

Roebuck & Co.
Norton Street, Leichardt, Sydney
1908–c.1945
(pp. 293,298–305)

Roebuck & Sons Pty Ltd, F
c.1945–72
(pp. 305–11)

Sloman and Son, C
Adelaide
1910
(p. 294)

Woolcock, C
Nr. Launceston,Tasmania
1980s–present day
(p. 340)

AUSTRIA

Anker, Josef
Spiel-Kunst Holzspielzeug
Mooshofe 16, A-6-74 Rinn/Tirol
1988
Hobby-horses and rocking horses
in natural wood finish.

Bauer, Ferdinand
Sautergasse 35, 1160 Vienna
1906–90
Hand-carved wooden rocking
horses
(Survey p. 5)

Gerngross, A
Vienna
1900

Kertesz, Heinrich
1 Fleischmarkt 9, Vienna
1900

Kober, Josef
1 Graben 14, Vienna
1868–c.1909
(pp. 209,211)

Kohler, K
Johnsdorf
1856–c.1910
(p. 209)

Kohn, Ignaz
Teplitz
1830–c.1920s
(pp. 27,209–10)

Niessner, Anton C
7/2 Kirchengasse Nr 9u, 9a
Vienna
1902
(pp. 209–12)

Pohl, Wilhelm
VI Mariahilferstrasse 5 and
I, Karntnerstrasse 39
Vienna
1854–c.1915
(p. 209)

BELGIUM

Beeusaert, Nazaire
Deinze
1920–90
(Survey p. 7)

Desiré, Dierick
14 Chausee de Gand
Peteghem, Deinze
1900–40
Rocking chairs, childrens' and
dolls' prams, tricycles and mail
carts. Close ties with Beeusaert.
(Survey p. 7)

De Vaux, Laurent
18th century
(p. 27)

Lemaire & Crenn
Mons
1900

**Van Kerk, Guillume or
Guillaume**
Schaerbeck
1900–40
Papier mâché horses in range of
sizes.

Veck
Brussels
1874–1955
Paper mâché horses in range of
sizes.

CANADA

Baillargé, Francois
Quebec
1759–1830
(Survey p. 29)

Berlin Woodenware Co.
20/22 Cedar, Ontario
1901–18
Founder D B Betzner. Made
rocking horses and household
goods.

Brocklin Toys Ltd
New Albany, Nova Scotia
1980–present day
Maple rocking horse with wooden
mane and tail designed by Brock
Savage in 1979.

Brokenshire, Silas
Fenelon Falls, Victoria
Ontario
1890
Wooden rocking horse on
platform, carved and painted.

Buzz Woodcrafts
3313 Church Street
Vancouver, British Columbia
1979–present day
Wooden horse on rockers
designed by Jim Pummell.

Chums & Co. Inc.
PO Box 356, Industrial Park
Althoville, New Brunswick
1982–present day
Wooden horse covered in mohair.

H C Toy Co.
1717 Gosfield Road
Kingsfield, Ontario
1973–90
Canadian pine horse on rockers designed by Larry R Neil. Leather ears and halter, synthetic fur mane and tail.

Headstrome Canada Inc.
185 King Street East
PO Box 3097, Cambridge
Ontario
1990 acquired Preston Manufacturing.

Hiker Manufacturing Co.
521 Esquimalt Road
Victoria, British Columbia
1919–38
Rocking horse, shooflies, and turkeys, roosters and swans.

Leblanc, Rosaire
Ste-Sophie-de-levard
Nicolet, Quebec

Lindner, Moritz
Berlin, Kitchener
Ontario
1881
(Survey pp. 31–3, 37)

Porcupine Opportunities Program
Box 697, Porcupine Plaine
Saskatchewan
1960s and 1970s
(Survey p. 32)

Taylor, Scott & Co.
Toronto, Ontario
1906–14
Made two sizes of shooflies.

CHINA

Education and Recreational Toy Factory
Beijing
1970s–present day
All kinds of rocking and bouncing toys in wood and plastic.

CZECHOSLOVAKIA

Exico Ltd
43 New North Road
London
Importer from Czechoslovakia
1980s–present day
Plush-covered horses on metal rockers, approx. 18 in. high.

DENMARK

Bøjesen, Kay
Bredgade 47, 1260 Copenhagen
1913–present day
(Survey pp. 25–26)

Lund, J J
Copenhagen
1800s
A saddler who also made horses.

Mathiasen, K E
Sintrupvej 12
DK–8220 Brabrand
1975–present day
Rocking horses and rocking horse seats. TM 'Lotte'.

Thorngreen, Theodor
Vimmdskafted 46
Copenhagen
19th century
Skin-covered horse in Folkmuseum Brede.

FINLAND

Aarikka
Nokiantie 2 - 4 c, SF–00510
Helsinki
1984–present day
(Survey p. 26)

Jussila Co., Juho
PO box 178
SF–40101 Jyvaskyla
1923–present day
TM 'Jukka'
(Survey p. 26)

FRANCE

André et Pichot
Ancenis, Loire Atlantique
1951
Wooden horses.

Arbre à Jouer
Raoul Lorge SA
PO Box 29, 39260 Vouglans
1870–present day
(Survey p. 10)

Aubin-Krier
Les Jouets Auxerrois
Auxerre, Yonne
1951
Wooden horses and toys.

Bayol, Gustave
Angers
c.1910–20s

Bazinet et Fils
90300 Champagnole, Jura
1922–53
Painted papier mâché and calfskin horses on rockers and wheeled platforms.

Blanchet
Chabernet-le-Pont-Chretien
36800 Saint Garnier
1953–present day
Plush-covered horses on rockers and wheels. In 1960s large horses and donkeys one metre high.

Bourgaie, Louis
Paris
1881
(p. 202)

Burlion, Paul
39 rue de Trois Bornes
Paris
1916–34
Wooden horses on platforms and rockers.
(Survey p. 47)

Clairbois
Avenue de Saint-Claude
39260 Moirans-en-Montagne
1880–present day
(Survey p. 10)

Clerc (Les Fils de N Clerc)
15 rue de Breteuil
60360 Crevecoeur-le-Grand, Oise
1900–30s
TM 'Pampo'
(Survey pp. 11, 46)

Colleville
36000 Chateauroux, Indre
1951
Painted and lacquered horses.

Cornu
124 rue de Montreuil
93230 Romainville, Seine
1887–present day
Wooden horses and other rocking animals until 1958 under TM 'Yam'.1963 taken over by plastics firm.

Coupey, Henri
59112 Annoeullin
Nord
1951
Wooden horses.

Courbé, M
1822 patent
(p. 196)

Didamat (ETB Roux, Patrick)
3 Allee des Echoppes
7716 Sauvigné le Temple
1980–present day
Simple wooden horses on rockers with wool or painted manes and see-saws with horses' heads on end seats.

Dumet, Gerard
63 Avenue des Celestins, Vichy
1980–present day
Wooden and plush horses.

Everaert, L
59066 Roubaix Nord
1951
Painted and lacquered wooden horse.

Fabrique Moderne de Jouets en Bois
81305 Graulhet, Tarn
1951
Very large wooden horses.

Favre
PO Box 3, 39260
Morans-en-Montagne
1974–present day
Part of Superjouet group. In 1974 made metal and plastic rocking toys.

Floch
Guer, 56380 Morbihan
Brittany
1950–78
Wooden rocking horses.

Fiot, Franck
9 rue des Castors
95710 Bray-et-Lu, Seine et Oise
1947–81

Gaidot, Rene
Bourg-les-Valence, Drome
1951
Flat cut-out wooden horses on rockers.

Garnier, A
58 rue de la Glacière, Paris
Factory at Caen, Normandy
1890–1922
Major manufaturer of rocking horses and tricycles, whose rear wheels had elaborate cast-iron supports.
(pp. 193–99, Survey pp. 9, 47)

Giraud-Sauveur, Leon
Champagnole
Jura
1910–present day
Pre-Second World War made traditional wooden horses and donkeys on bow rockers and wheeled platforms. 1960s still advertised wooden as well as compostion and plastic horses.
(Survey p. 10)

Giraudon, F
Bouin, Vendee
1951
Wooden rocking horses.

Gourdoux, Jean Louis
Paris
1821 patent.
(p. 196)

Grelety, Guy
17500 Jonzac, Charrente Maritime
1950–present day
TM 'Gy-Gy' and pony's head.Pastel painted wooden cut-out horses and more elaborate plush-covered stuffed horses. In 1990 their show-jumping pony won Oscar award of French Toy Industry.

Gros, Y
3002 Clermont-Ferrand
1951
Wooden rocking horses.

Guiton, M
13–17 Passage Jouffroy, Paris
1875
(p. 198)

Hamon, Georges
La Croix-les-Rochelettes
Les Course, Fougeres
1951
Wooden rocking horses.

Lang
01220 Divonne les Baines
Ain
1924–78
TM 'FADAP' (Fabrique d'Animaux en Peluche). Plush-covered horses and donkeys on metal rockers, wheels and tricycles.

Lefèvre, Gilbert
Paris XV
1951
Wooden rocking horses.

La Sauterelle
Route de l'Eglise
37500 Candes St Martin, Chinon
1990–present day
(Survey p. 11)

Le Derby
La Varenne-Saint-Hilaire
1951
Wooden rocking horses.

Lenoble
60300 Senlis, Oise
1899–1930
(p. 127, Survey pp. 10–11, 46)

Les Ateliers du Pere Noel
93140 Bondy, Seine
1951
Painted wooden horses.

Manning, Charles E
21 rue des Orties, Colombes
Nr Paris
Late 19th century
(pp. 132, 201, 229)

Maxime, Charles
rue Pasteur
72500 Chateau du Loire, Sarthe
1951–62
Wooden horses on platforms and
rockers.

Nicodème
77400 Dampart, Seine-et-Marne
1951
Horses on rockers and platforms.
(Survey p. 47)

Noe
Villecien, Yonne
1963
Plush ponies, horses and other
animals on wheels and metal
rockers.

Nounours
Le Rocher Bidaine
3520 Chatillon-en-Vendelais
1963–present day
Variety of plush-covered animals
on metal or wooden rockers
convertible to wheeled toys.

Peter Pan
132 rue du Moulin à Vent
93105 Montreuil, Seine
1950–54
Painted and lacquered horses on
wheels and rockers.

Philllippeau
Hautes, Loire Atlantique
1951
TM 'Philo'. Horses and donkeys
in lacquered wood.

Pintel
4–6 Avenue du Trone
Paris
1920–63
TM 'Snaiflex'.
Wide range of plush animals on
metal rockers.

Serret, Remy
23 rue Curaterie, 26200
Montelimar
1985–present day
Remy Serret comes from a family
of traditional wood carvers and, as
well as portraits, puppets and
other carvings, he makes rocking
horses to order from lime, walnut
or cypress.
(Survey p. 11)

S I D A F
(Societe Industrielle de
Decorations et Articles Fantasie)
3 rue Charles de Gaulle
42022 St. Etienne, Loire
1936–71
Plush-covered horses on wheels
and rockers.

Taiga
10240 Ramerupt
1980–1990
Hand-carved English-style,
limewood horses on safety rockers
with horse hair tails and sculpted
manes, 97 cm and 112 cm high.
(Survey p. 11)

Villet Frères
PO Box 10
39260 Moirans-en-Montagne
1939–present day
TM 'Vilac'. Current horses are
called 'Stormy' and are painted or
lacquered wood.

GERMANY

Ahrens, Christine
D–4830 Gutersloh 1
Arndtstrasse 47
1990
Simple wooden horse designed by
H & C Wiechert.

Alpenlandische Wohnkultur
Grunwalder Weg 14
8025 Unterhacking
1990
Pine horse on cradle rockers,
painted outline.

Alt & Koch
Weidigsmuchle
1876
(p. 135)

Anker Mechanik, VEB
Eisfeld
19th century –1952 and
1976–present day
(pp. 173,179,183–85)

Bauer & Krause
Leipzig
c.1880–c.1930
(pp. 127, 135–37, 140, 145, 154,
158–59, 162, 167–70, 172, 178,
181–82, 236, 262)

Becht, Gudrun
Schutzenring 29, 2260 Niebull
(Survey p. 14)

Beck, Carl & Schulze, Alfred
Ohrdruf, Thuringia
1878–1933
(pp. 135, 138, 140, 143, 160)

Beir, Osc
Waldkirchen, Thuringia
Listed in 1929

Beilstein, Fritz
Niederhausen, Odenwald
1900–59
Barrel-shaped horses.

**Berchtesgadener
Handwerkskunst**
Schroffenbergallee 6
8240 Berchtesgaden
1990/ or present day
Wooden rocking horse.

Bier, Fritz
Eisfeld
c.1920–52
(p. 173)

Bier, Hermann
Eisfeld
c.1920–52
(p. 173)

Biggi, VEB
Waltershausen, Thuringia
1972–present day
(pp. 140, 145, 149–52, 154, 157,
169, 236)

Bischof, Reinhold
Thuringia
1947

Dressel, Cuno & Otto
Nuremberg and Sonneberg
Thuringia
1805–1930
Rocking horses, marbles and
wooden toys.

Feldbacher, Thomas
Piho toys
Pinzgauer Holzspeilzeug, Rosental
144
A–5741 Neukirchen am
Grossvenediger
1990 or present day
Three sizes of rocking horses with
adjustable footrests.

Fischer, Ruan
Kohlenhausen 20
2161 Ahlerstedt
1990/present day
Two sizes of wooden horse and a
hobby horse.

Florschutz, Johannes
Eisfeld, Thuringia
1920s
(p. 173)

Freitag & Co., F W
10 Arnstaedter Strasse
Ohrdruf, Thuringia
Later Thuringian Toy Company
1878–1907
(pp. 135–37, 143)

Glenk, Frederick
Odenwald
1900

Gottschalk, Moritz
Marienburg, Erzgebirge
1929

Graeffer, Felix
Schleiz, Thuringia
1876–1929
(pp. 138, 142, Survey p. 46)

Grob, Carl
Eblingen, Baden-Wurtemberg
1929

Guyot, Adam
Rohrback, Odenwald
1907–38
(Survey p. 14)

Hauber O U M
Ludwigsburg
1929

Hofmann, Ernest EWH Design
Weiserlerstrasse 102 (B3)
6308, Butzback
1990
Wooden horses and other animals.

Horst Meier
Waldstrasse 32, D 07129
Zaberfeld 1
1950–present day
(p. 183)

Jäger & Co.
Ohrdruf, Thuringia
1879–29
(pp. 135,138)

Kahn & Co., Leopold
Schwabish,Gmund
1929
Plush-covered four-wheeled horse,
pedal action propulsion.
(Survey p. 46)

Keitel, Otto
Ohrdruf, Thuringia
1929–34
(p. 140)

**Keller Konrad
Holzspielwarenfabrik**
Metzgerstr. 6, D–7320 Goppingen
1978

Knauth, Edmund
Orlamunde, Thuringia
1890–1947
Fabric and skin-covered animals,
rocking and wheeled horses.

Knoll, Julius
Gorlitz-Leschwitz
1929
Wooden toys and animal rocking
seats.

Krämer, Adam
Reichelsheim, Odenwald
1899–1990
(Survey pp. 13–14)

Kuhnelt & co.
Lauenstein
Listed in 1929

Kurtz, Hermann
Stuttgart
1912
Horses on rockers, platforms and
rollers as well as hobby horses.

Leonhardt, Paul
Eppendorf
1929
Wooden toys and stables.

Loffler, Alfred
Sachsbrunn, Eisfeld
c.1915–c.1960
(p. 173)

Loffler, Rudolph
Sachsbrunn, Eisfeld
c.1950–present day
(pp. 173–75,178)

Meinung & Co., C E
Ohrdrufer Felltier und
Holzspeilwarenfabrik
Ohrdruf, Thuringia
1835–29
(p. 135, Survey p. 46)

Müller, B A
Dresden
Early 20th century
(p. 131)

Necke
Bahnhofstrasse 8
D–8621 Schneckenlohe

Opel & Kühne
Zeitz, Thuringia
1929

Prüfer & Co., Otto
Zeitz, Thuringia
1929
(Survey p. 47)

Richter & Wittich
Eppendorf
1929

Rissland & Sohne, Hugo
Gillersdorf
Grossbreitenbach, Thuringia
1929
(p. 142)

Robert, Martin
Dittersbach
1929

Roithner & Co., Hugo
Schweidnitz, Silesia
1929
(Survey p. 47)

Schmalfuss, C F
Schneeberg, Saxony
(pp. 138, 142)

Schmohl, Gebr.
Goppingen, Wurtemberg
1929
TM 'Gesgo'
(pp. 138, 143)

Schneider, Franz
Siemenstrasse 13–19
D 8623 Neustadt-bei-Coburg
Present day
Plush horses on wooden rockers
and fluffy horse seats on metal
rockers and wheels.

Schöbel, Arno & Gustav
Lossau bei Schleiz, Thuringia
1929
(Survey p. 47)

Schowanek
1980s–present day
(p. 23)

Schütz, Mathias
1674
(p. 125)

Steiff, Margarete, GmbH
Giengen-an-der-Brenz
1880–present day
(pp. 186–92)

Stukenbrok, August
Einbeck
1912
Plush and skin-covered platform
rocking horses. (Survey p. 46)

**'Superior' Fahrrad und
Maschinen Industrie**
Eisenach, Thuringia
1908
(p. 149)

Sudthuringer Spielwarenwerke
Eisfeld
1952–76
(p. 173)

Thuringian Toy Company
Ohrdruf, Thuringia
1907–1930s
Formerly F W Freitag & Co.
(pp. 23, 136, 138–40, 146, 152–54,
157, 159–60, 168–71, 176, 178,
183)

Vertriebs-Gesellschaft Seiffen
Erzgebirge
1929
Wooden horses.

Wagner & Sohne, D H
Grunhainichen, Saxony
1742–1920s
(pp. 26, 138, 142)

Wahnschaffe, A
Nuremberg
1895
Skin-covered horses on bow
rockers, wheels and platforms.
(Survey p. 46)

Werner, Anton
Grundleinsweg 1
8620 Lichtenfels, Schney
1978
Wooden chair horses.

Wertheim, A
Berlin West 66
1904
Advertised horse and goat on bow
rockers, stables with horses and
carts, and boxed sets of horse and
stable equipment.

Zoo Werkstatten
Munich
1920s
(pp. 62–3)

HUNGARY

Keistof, Nagy
Budapest
1970s–1980s
(Survey pp. 16–17)

ITALY

Canova, Giocattoli
Casalserugo, Padua
1970s
Plush and plastic rocking horses.

Insam & Prinoth
Ortisei
1880s–c.1914
(Survey pp. 19–20)

Perego Pines
Via de Gasperi 50
20043 Arcore, Milan
1991
'Rocky' coin-in-the-slot modern
horse

Sevi
Casella Postale 44, 1–39046
Ortesei
1831–present day
(Survey pp. 18–19)

Trudi Geocattoli SPA
via Angelo Angleti 120
1–33017 Tarcento
1990/present day
Soft toys on rockers.

NORWAY

Bausback, Georg
19 Graendsey Kristiana
1915
(p. 208)

Husfliden
Mollergt 4, 0179 Oslo
1990

Lunde, T H
Listed in Crafts cooperative
Catalogue of 1930 as making
horses on cradle rockers and bow
rockers, shooflies and horse seats
on wheels.

Jorgensen, K A
Oslo
1920
Catalogue shows various types of
wooden rocking horses.

PHILIPPINES

Gerard Heiner
4 Forestry Street
Vaasra Village
Project 60c
Manila

POLAND

Bartnau, Kazimerz
Brzozow woj, Rzeszów
1967
Wooden rocking horses, painted
with oil paint and decorated with
geometrical designs.

Bogdal, Jan
Harbutowice woj, Cracow
1976
Wooden rocking horses, decorated
with flowers and geometrical
designs.

Buszta, Jozef
37–109 Brzoza Stadnicka 98
Rzeszów
Wooden, flat, seated rocking
horses decorated with leaves and
spots.

Ciszek, Stanislaw
Ostojow 190,
Woj. Kielce
1974
Wooden rocking horse, painted
geometric designs. Rabbits' fur
mane, leather ears, horsehair tail.

Gajewski, Jozef
Wielkie Radowiska
1957
Wooden horses with flat seat.

Guzy, Stanislaw
37–109 Brozoza Stadnicka
Rzeszów
1975
Wooden rocking horses with
carved mane and tail, decorated
with spots

Hodurek, Jozef
1975
Wooden horses on platforms and
wooden wheels.

Lorenc, Jozef
37–109 Brzoza Stadnicka 11,
Rzeszów
Painted wooden rocking horse on
rockers.

Narog, Stanislaw
37–110 Zolynia 76
Rzeszów
Painted wooden rocking horses,
decorated with flower designs.
Five sizes.
(Survey p. 22)

SPAIN

Falgas
Figueres, Gerona
Present day
(Survey p. 20)

SWEDEN

Brio Leksaksfabrik

Bröderna Ivarsson
Osby
1907–present day
(p. 208)

Engquist, Olof W
Flen
1920s and 1930s
(p. 206)

**Gemla Leksaksfabriks
Aktiebolags**
Gemla and later Dio
1866–1892
Gemla
1892–1954
(pp. 206–08

SWITZERLAND

**Erste Schweizerische
Speilwarenfabrik**
c.1900
(p. 125)

Fahrni and Co.
Rothrist, Aargau
1900–14
(Survey p. 27)

Strehler, Gebr.
Wald
c.1920
(Survey p. 27)

Würgler, Rudolf
PO Box 8911, CH 3001 Bern
1986–present day
(Survey pp. 27–28)

UNITED KINGDOM AND
IRELAND

Ajoy Ltd
24 Silk Street, London
1924

Allen, John
3 Clarence Place
Hackney, London
1838
(p. 46)

Allison, John
17 Charlotte Terrrace
New Cut, London
1822
(p. 46)

Ayres, Frederick Henry
111 Aldersgate Street
London
1864–1940
(pp. 41, 47, 54, 61–2, 65–77,
298–99, 302)

Baby Carriages Ltd
165/67 Duke Street, Liverpool
1884–1958
(p. 118)

Bashall, Betty
8 Queen's Drive
Thames Ditton, Surrey
1930–38

Brassington & Cooke
Cable Street, Manchester
1875–1930s

Burrow, G C
1862 Patent
(p. 60)

Carlton, Richard
6 Webber Street
New Cut, London
1838
(p. 46)

Chiltern Toys
1920s and 1930s
See Stone & Co., H G

Chinn & McMillen
23 St. James Road
Kingston, Surrey
1920

C M T Wells Kelo Ltd
Progress Works
Kingsland, Holyhead
Gwynedd LL65 2 SN
1970–present day

Collinson & Son, J
463 Smithdown Road
Liverpool
1836–present day
(pp. 39, 46–7, 57, 91, 117–23)

Como Enterprises
Stourbridge
Worcestershire
1973–77

Davies & Co., Alfred
Penn Road Works
Caledonian Road
Holloway, London N7
1895–1923

Dean's Rag Book Co. Ltd
London
1927–present day

De La Rue, Evelyn
1906 Patent
(p. 62)

Dew, Anthony
Holme-Upon-Spalding Moor
York
1970s–present day
(p. 357)

Dobby Horse Exploitation
Syndicate
38 Parliament Street
Whitehall, London
1922

Edinburgh Toy Factory Ltd
121–23 Fountainbridge Road
Edinburgh
1916

Elite Toy Manufacturing Co.
Salt Street Manningham
Bradford, Yorks
1916

Farnell, J K
Alpha Works
Acton Hill, London
1962

Franke, Bertram E Jones
London Works
Wellesley Street
Hockley, Birmingham
1912–32

Fryer & Co. (Nelson) Ltd
Victory Factories
Nelson, Lancs
1946

Fryland
165 Sherlock Street
Birmingham
1915

Gabriel, William
9 Ward's Court
Goswell Street, London
1784
(p. 36)

Galway Toy Industry
Earls Island
Galway, Ireland
1920

Goodwood Toys
Lavant, Chichester
1964–73

Gordon Crafts Ltd
Gordon Works
Alder Road
Poole, Dorset
1946–49

Honey & Co., James
Beckenham Road
Penge, London
1914

Hooper Ltd, H S
54 Great Eastern Street
London
1916–25

Kain (late Jones)
25 Ludgate Street, London
Early 19th century
(p. 36)

Keith Lowe Engineers Ltd
Dudley
1963–1970

Kendrick, R & F W
Bedford Street, Loughborough
1920

Kennedy, William Sadler
Middlesex
1861 Patent
(p. 60)

Kirby
Lower Sackville Street and
O'Connell Street
Dublin
(p. 46)

Kiss, David & Noreen
Wem, Shropshire
1980s–present day
(pp. 76, 356, 361)

Leach, P
305 Euston Road, London
19th century
(p. 36)

Lefray Toys Ltd.
Aberbeeg
Gwent
1989–present day

Lines, G & J
Bagnidge Wells
King's Cross, London
1850–1876
457 Caledonian Road
1876–1913 and
Thistle Works, Tottenham
1913–31
(pp. 39, 41, 47, 49, 52, 54–8, 61,
78–101, 118, 120, 169, 275, 281,
293–94, 313, 332)

Lines Bros Ltd
Ormside Street
Old Kent Road, London
1919–21
Tri-ang Works
761 Old Kent Road
1921–24
Morden Road
Merton, Surrey
1924–72
Use of Tri-ang mark from 1927
(pp. 102, 111, 258, 262, 305, 307)

Liverpool Toy Industry
6 Soho Street, Liverpool
1924
(p. 118)

Luckett & Sons, Thomas
Mark Lane, Petershore
Birmingham
1890–1029

Marriott, John
Bedfordshire
1980s–present day
(p. 357)

Merrythought Ltd
Dale End, Iron Bridge
Shropshire
1938–present day
(pp. 19, 24)

Mettamake Ltd
444 New Chester Road
Rock Ferry, Liverpool
1928

Midland Tent & Strong Toy Co.
Imperial Works
129 Duddeston Mill road,
Birmingham
1909

Norton & Baker
Victory Works
Horse Fair, Birmingham
1890–1920s

Novel Toy Manufacturing Co.
50a Birch Lane, Longsight
Manchester
1920

Palmer, Stephen
26 Hackney Road, London
1822
(p. 46)

Palser, Samuel
30 Webber Row
Waterloo Road, London
1838

Patterson Edwards
Old Kent Road, London
1892–1975

R H Manufacturing Co.
26 Wellington Street
The Strand, London
1922

Ragamuffin Toys
Feremina, St Martin's
Guernsey, Channel Islands
1976–81
England
1988–present day
(p. 266)

Ray Delfi
14 Lidiard Road
Earlsfield, London
1973
(p. 105)

Relko
Devon and later
New Zealand
1970s–present day
(p. 357)

Scott & Walker Ltd
Birmingham
1915–26

Sebel & Co. Ltd, D
Kent
1940s–70s
(pp. 112–15)

Selcol
114 Charing Cross Road
London
1962

Sharna-Tri-ang Ltd
Manchester
1972–present day
(p. 109)

Shillelagh Wood Industries
Shillelagh, Ireland
1915

Smith, J R & T
96 Downham Road
Kingsland, London
1886–1916
(p. 15)

Spencer, Margaret
Somerset
1970s–present day
(p. 357)

Spooner, Charles John
(Orton & Spooner)
Swan works, Meadow Road
Trent Bridge, Burton-on-Trent
1890

Star Manufacturing Co.
Davis Street
Cubbitt Town, London
1908–1920s?

Star Yacht Works
Marion Street
Birkenhead
1934

Stevenson Brothers
Kent
1982–present day
(pp. 358–60)

Stone & Co., H G
New Union Street, London
1920–30s
Brand names 'Chiltern' and
'Panurge Pets'
(pp. 16–17)

Taylor, John & James
2 Shoemaker's Row
Blackfriars, London
1822
(pp. 36, 46)

Usher & Co. Ltd, J
4 Back Guildford Street
Everton Road, Liverpool
1909

Vickers Ltd
Vickers House
Broadway, London
1920

Victor Aviation Toy Co.
Type Street
Old Ford, London
1919–1920s

Welsh Toy Industry
Crwys Bridge, Cardiff
1919

Whiley Brothers Ltd
Jubilee Place, Leeds and
110 Kew Green
Richmond, Surrey
1854–1930s
(pp. 49, 56)

Wilson & Son Ltd
Silver Cross Works
Leeds
1880–1920s
(p. 91)

Woodrow & Co. Ltd, G
Swallow Works
683 High Road
Tottenham
London
1933–1950s

Woods, John and Dorothy
Bolton
1976–present day
(p. 358)

Cheval.

Carton moulé sur bascule
démontable.
Nos 4 à 8.
Haut. 54 à 79 %m.

« Au galop ».
Cheval bois laqué basculant et roulant,
avec poignées.
Nos 16 à 19 — Haut. 60 à 77 %m.

Cheval.

Bois laqué sur plateau.
Nos B/3/0 à B/4 — Haut. 37 à 73 %m.

ABOVE *Papier mâché and wooden
horses advertised by Clerc in 1938.*

ABOVE RIGHT AND RIGHT
*Skin-covered wheeled and rocking
horses by Lenoble.*

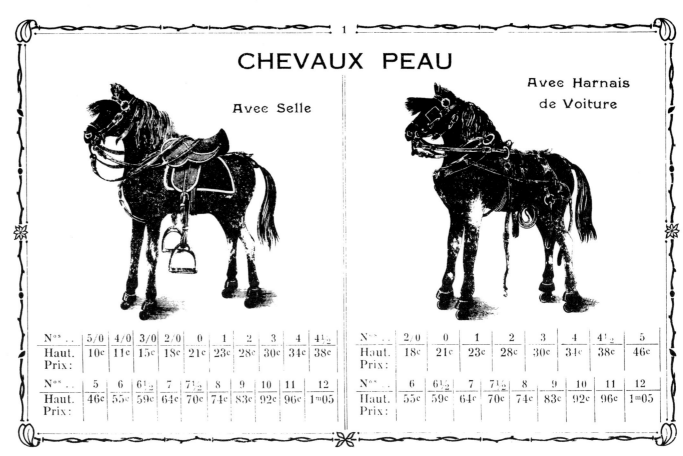

1

CHEVAUX PEAU

Avec Selle

Avec Harnais
de Voiture

Nos	5/0	4/0	3/0	2/0	0	1	2	3	4	4½
Haut.	10c	11c	15c	18c	21c	23c	28c	30c	34c	38c
Prix:										

Nos	5	6	6½	7	7½	8	9	10	11	12
Haut.	46c	55c	59c	64c	70c	74c	83c	92c	96c	1m05
Prix:										

Nos	2/0	0	1	2	3	4	4½	5
Haut.	18c	21c	23c	28c	30c	34c	38c	46c
Prix:								

Nos	6	6½	7	7½	8	9	10	11	12
Haut.	55c	59c	64c	70c	74c	83c	92c	96c	1m05
Prix:									

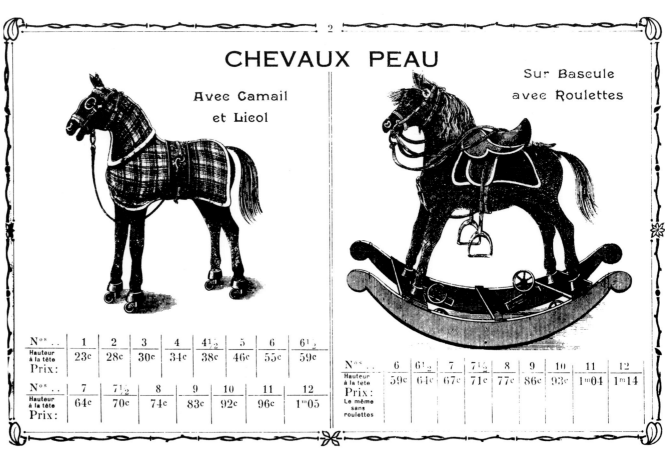

2

CHEVAUX PEAU

Avec Camail
et Licol

Sur Bascule
avec Roulettes

Nos	1	2	3	4	4½	5	6	6½
Hauteur à la tête Prix:	23c	28c	30c	34c	38c	46c	55c	59c

Nos	7	7½	8	9	10	11	12
Hauteur à la tête Prix:	64c	70c	74c	83c	92c	96c	1m05

Nos	6	6½	7	7½	8	9	10	11	12
Hauteur à la tête Prix: Le même sans roulettes	59c	64c	67c	71c	77c	86c	93c	1m04	1m14

GRANDE FABRIQUE DE VOITURES
POUR ENFANTS · & MALADES

ETABLISᵗˢ A. GARNIERᵒ

SOCIÉTÉ AU CAPITAL DE 1.100.000 FRANCS

58, Rue de la Glacière - PARIS (13ᵉ)

Téléph. : Gobelins 04 52

MARQUE DÉPOSÉE
ARTICLE FRANÇAIS
Numéro 152

Métro : Glacière

GRAND PRIX, Exposition de Londres. — GRAND PRIX, Exposition Internationale et Nationale 1897. — DIPLOME D'HONNEUR, Exposition de l'Enfance Paris 1901. — MÉDAILLE D'ARGENT, Exposition 1900 (O) (A) Paris et Rouen. — MÉDAILLE D'OR, Exposition Saint-Louis 1904. — Exposition Bruxelles 1910 DIPLOME D'HONNEUR. — Turin 1911, GRAND PRIX. — Gand 1913, GRAND PRIX, — Lyon 1914, GRAND PRIX. — San-Francisco 1915, HORS CONCOURS.

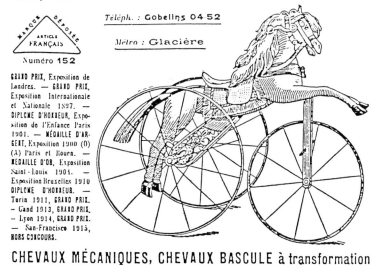

CHEVAUX MÉCANIQUES, CHEVAUX BASCULE à transformation

Spécialiste du Cheval de Bois
ANIMAUX HUMORISTIQUES A BASCULE
Selles et fauteuils en moleskine souple, roues caout-choutées permettant le roulement silencieux.
NOTRE SYSTÈME DOUBLE USAGE LE PLUS SIMPLE (déposé) JOLIS DÉCORS

R. NICODÈME
TÉLÉPH. : 13   DAMPMART   (SEINE-ET-MARNE)

SALLE D'ÉCHANTILLONS A PARIS :
M. PAUTARD
7, Rue du Grand Prieuré — Tél. : VOL. 01-50 — Métro : Oberkampf

ABOVE *Advertisement from Annuaire Jeux et Jouets, 1922*

LEFT *A Garnier advertisement from 1922 cataogue. (Musée des Arts Decoratives Archives)*

FABRIQUE DE JOUETS EN BOIS
et de Charrettes pour Enfants

MARQUE DÉPOSÉE
ARTICLE FRANÇAIS
Numéro 112

PAUL BURLION

39, Rue des Trois-Bornes — PARIS (11ᵉ)

Métro : PARMENTIER

TÉLÉPHONE :
ROQUETTE
58.62

Jouets roulants en hêtre : Brouettes, Tombereaux, Charrettes.
Tables et Chaises fixes et pliantes.
Chevaux bois sur plateau et sur bascule démontable.

Paul Burlion advertisement from 1922 catalogue. (Musée des Arts Decoratives Archives)

A Beck & Schultz horse advertised in Games and Toys, *August 1923.*

Rocking horse from A Stukenbrok's 1912 catalogue.

Wheeled horse from H. Kurt's 1912 catalogue.

Gmünder Stoffspielwarenfabrik

LEOPOLD KAHN & Co.

Schwäb. Gmünd

FABRIK FEINER PLÜSCHSPIELWAREN

NEUHEIT:

Fahrtiere als Selbstfahrer

ges. geschützt

Zur Messe in Leipzig: Zentralmeßpalast

Neumarkt 2-4, IV. Obergeschoß Nr. 341-348

Ohrdrufer Felltier- und Holzspielwarenfabrik

Meinung & Co. G. m. b. H., Ohrdruf in Thüringen

Spezialitäten:

Feinste Felltiere

Schaukelpferde / Schafe / Ziegen

Feinste Schiebwagen

Jagdwagen / Rollwagen / Karren
Pferdeställe usw.

Spezialitäten:

Kinderautos, Spielautos

aller Art in reichster Auswahl

Polichinelle-Figuren

umfassendes Sortiment aller Charaktertypen

Kinderreifen / Geburtstagsringe
Füllartikel / Osterartikel

Zu den Messen in Leipzig: Zentralmeßpalast, 4. Obergeschoß, Zimmer 96

ABOVE LEFT *Horses offered by A Wahnschaffe of Nuremberg, 1895 catalogue.*

ABOVE RIGHT, CENTER AND BELOW *Three advertisements from* Deutsche Spielwaren-Zeitung, *1929*

Otto Prüfer & Co.
Zeitz 2, Thür.
HOLZSPIELWAREN - FABRIK
Gegründet 1889
Zur Messe in Leipzig: Petershof,
V. Obergeschoß, Zimmer 523 b
*
Wir fabrizieren konkurrenzl. billig:
Kinderschaukeln in 10 Aus-
tührungen, **Holzautos, Eisen-
bahnen,** Fahrbare und beweg-
liche Tiere, Gespanne, letztere aus
3 fachem, verleimten Sperrholz,
daher unzerbrechlich

Arno & Gustav Schöbel
Spielwarenfabrik
Lössau bei Schleiz (Thüring.)

Spezialität:

**Holz-, Fell-,
Plüsch-, Fahr- u.
Schaukelpferde
div. Gespanne**

Zur
Messe in Leipzig:
**Messpalast
Specks-Hof, Zimmer 565
III. Etage**

Musterlager in **Berlin S 42:** G. F. Hertzog & Co., Ritterstraße 31
Leipzig S 3: Karl Kraul, Scheffelstraße 38

Thüringer Spielwarenfabrik
vorm. F. W. Freitag & Co. G.m.b.H. Ohrdruf, Thür.

Ab diesjähriger

Frühjahrsmesse

in Leipzig finden Sie
unsere reichhaltige Ausstellung von

**Spiel- und Schaukelpferden, Fell-, Plüsch- und Stofftieren,
Pferdeställen, Fuhrwerken sowie Spiel- und Sport-Autos
im neuen „Petershof", 4. Obergeschoß,** Zimmer 455-57
(Petersstraße)

*Horse-head chair roundabout by
Hugo Roithner, advertised in
Deutsche Spielwaren-Zeitung,
1929.*

*Rocking horse from A. Wertheim's
1904 catalogue.*

No. 8249.   Schaukelpferde, m. Naturfell. M. 6.75, 9.75 bis 34.-
mit imitiertem Fell . . . . M. 4.25, 6.—, 8.75

Bibliography

BOOKS

Baschet, Eric: Les Inventions Extraordinaires, *Archives de l'Illustration, Paris, 1981.*

Burckhardt, Monica: Le Jouet de Bois, *Fleurus. Paris, 1987.*

D'Allemagne, H R: Histoire des Jouets et Recreations et Passetemps. *Hatchette, Paris, 1905.*

Daiken, Leslie: Children's Toys Throughout the Ages. *Batsford, London, 1952.*

Dew, Anthony: Making Rocking Horse. *David & Charles, Newton Abbott, 1984.*

Fawdry, M: English Rocking Horses, *Pollock's Toy Theatres, London, 1986.*

Fawdry, K & M: Pollock's History English Toys and Dolls. *Ernest Benn, London, 1979.*

Flick, Pauline: Discovering Toys and Toy Museum. *Shire Publications, 1971.*

Fraser, Antonia: A History of Toys. *Weidenfeld & Nicolson, London, 1966.*

Herman, Paul: Le Jouet en Belgique. *Rossel, Brussels, 1984.*

King, Constance E: The Encyclopedia of Toys. *Robert Hale, London, 1978.*

Matheos, José Corredor: El Juguete en España. *Espassa Calpe. Madrid, 1989.*

Mayhew, Henry: Articles in the Morning Chronicle *25 February 1856.*

Milano, Alberta: Balocchi. *La Editoriale Libraria. Trieste 1985.*

Murray, Patrick: Toys. *Studio Vista, 1986.*

McClintock, Marshall & Inez: Toys in America. *Public Affairs Press, Washington, 1961.*

Ovsyannikov, Y. Russian Folk Arts and Crafts. *Progress Publishers, Moscow.*

Sequin, Robert Lionel: Les Jouets Anciens du Canada. *Lemeac. Quebec. 1976.*

Shishido, Misako: Folk Toys of Japan. *Japan Publications Trading Co. Rutland, Vermont. 1963.*

Sigsgaard, Jens: Old Toys in Denmark. *Arnold Busck. 1982. Det legede vi med gammelt legetoy Denmark.*

Stäblein, Rita: Altes Holzspielzeug aus Gröden. *Athesia. Bolzano. 1980.*

Stille, Eva: Spielzeug-Tiere. *Hans Carl. Nurenburg, 1989.*

Symons, Harry: Playthings of Yesterday. *Ryerson Press, Toronto, 1963.*

White, Gwen: Antique Toys and Their Background. *Batsford, London, 1971.*

MAGAZINES AND CATALOGUES

Black horses, Red Flowers. *(Gorodets art) Booklet published by Beriozka Chain of Shops.*

Canadian Encyclopedia. *Article by Janet Holmes.*

Deutsche Spielwaren-Zeitung. *Catalogues February 1929 and May 1929. Berlin-Nuremberg.*

Gamage's Christmas Bazaar 1913. *Reprint David & Charles. Newton Abbott, 1974.*

Handicrafts of India. *Indian Council for Cultural Relations.*

Jouets et Jeux. *Catalogues French Toy Manufacturers Editions Productions Publicitaires. Paris 1952–1990.*

Sicilian Handicrafts. *Salvatore Sciascia. Rome 1966.*

Toys. Dolls. Games. Catalogues 1903–1914. *Paris Stores Denys Ingram (now New Cavendish Books). London 1981.*

Waterloo County Times. *Article by Thomas Reitz. 1990.*